Planning **THE ORGANIC FLOWER GARDEN**

Explains how to make the most of flowers in any garden and grow them the organic way – including essential advice about planning, choosing for lasting colour and scent and suiting plants to the site.

Also in this series
PLANNING THE ORGANIC HERB GARDEN
   by Sue Stickland
PLANNING THE ORGANIC VEGETABLE GARDEN
   by Dick Kitto

By the same author
COMPOSTING
   by Dick Kitto

Planning
THE ORGANIC
FLOWER GARDEN

For All-Year-Round Colour

by

SUE STICKLAND

Line illustrations by Nils Solberg

THORSONS PUBLISHING GROUP

First published 1986

British Library Cataloguing in Publication Data

Stickland, Sue
Planning the organic flower garden: for
all-year-round colour.
1. Plants, Ornamental   2. Flower gardening
I. Title
635.9   SB404.9

ISBN 0-7225-1163-9

*Published by Thorsons Publishers
Limited, Wellingborough,
Northamptonshire*

Printed in Great Britain by Woolnough Bookbinding Limited,
Irthlingborough, Northamptonshire

3 5 7 9 10 8 6 4 2

CONTENTS

ACKNOWLEDGEMENTS

Many thanks are due to the following for letting me take photographs in their gardens:

Mr R. Seelig, Upton House, Tetbury, Glos. (Plates 2, 3, 5, 7, 9, 16). Mrs B. Shuker and Miss P. Strange, Yew Tree Cottage, Ampney St Mary, Glos. (Plate 1). Mrs A. Biddulph, Rodmarton Manor, Nr Cirencester, Glos. (Plate 12, 13). Mr and Mrs P. Harford, Great Somerford, Wilts. (Plate 14). Major and Mrs P. Phillips, Great Somerford, Wilts. (Plates 10, 11, 15). Mr and Mrs J. Sturgis, Dauntsey Park, Chippenham, Wilts. (Plate 8). Mrs. Bayliss, The Manor, Great Somerford, Wilts. (Plate 4).

Also to the Royal National Rose Society for their advice (Tables 15, 19) and to Mrs C. Stickland for the typing.

CHAPTER 1
THE IDEAL FLOWER GARDEN

Few would deny the pleasure that flowers bring: they tempt the reluctant gardener, inspire the beginner and provide endless scope for the enthusiast! Admittedly there are many other elements in an attractively designed garden: evergreen shrubs, foliage plants and ground cover plants, for example. But flowers offer so much more. They invite you to sniff them and examine them closely; to gather them up and bring their fresh colour indoors. They are also the main attraction for bees, butterflies, moths and the other pollen and nectar feeding insects which are an important part of garden life.

In the ideal garden, the flowers each contribute many individual qualities, while at the same time fitting in with their surroundings to present a pleasing overall effect. Ideally, too, all the plants should be thriving, whatever the garden is like. This is not just a summer afternoon's dream, as nature readily testifies: wild flowers appear unasked and uncared for in the most inhospitable places because they are well adapted to these situations. Similarly, cultivated plants must be chosen to suit the conditions in your garden, whether it is sunny or shady, marshy or dry. Visit other gardens to see how the plants are growing, rather than picking them out from pictures in a catalogue or from potted-up collections in a nursery.

Nature also shows how plants can be kept healthy. They should not be considered in isolation, but as part of the garden as a whole. This includes the soil and all the plant and animal inhabitants: the microscopic fungi and bacteria, worms and insects, birds and mammals, and even the weeds. Chemicals should be avoided as they upset the ecology of the garden. Pesticides and fungicides harm beneficial creatures more than their targets, causing an increase in pests and diseases in the long run. Artificial fertilizers cause lush growth at the expense of blooms and this encourages pest and disease attack. Weedkillers leave harmful deposits and weaken garden plants. Instead, weeds and plant debris should be returned to the soil as compost, which nourishes the soil organisms, so encouraging new plant growth. This 'organic' method of gardening is not an unworkable ideal, although it does involve more understanding and appreciation of garden life.

This book aims to help you plan your garden with all these ideals in mind. First come some questions you should ask about your garden and the plants you might grow – they should give you a basis on which to start planning. Chapter 2 covers the preparation of the site and how to care for the garden 'organically' after it has been planted; it contains a reference section of pests and diseases and their control. Chapter 3 is similarly a reference chapter for those who want to propagate their own plants

– this may be an important factor in planning a garden on a limited budget.

Each of Chapters 4 – 7 deals with a familiar type of plant – annuals, biennials, bulbs, herbaceous plants, etc. – and outlines how you might use them, and the growing conditions they need. Information is provided on their particular qualities, such as lasting colour, scent and resistance to disease. The emphasis is on plants that are hardy and not highly bred. You do not need a greenhouse to overwinter them, although this is always useful for propagation.

The last section in each of Chapters 4–7 gives a full description of the plants used in the plans in Chapter 8. These plans are not rigid patterns, but aim to show how and why flowering plants fit into different types of garden. The individual plants covered are all worthwhile growing – but they are by no means the only ones. There are many others that would qualify equally for a place in your own schemes.

Questions to ask about the garden

What type of soil does it have?
Is it exposed or sheltered?
Is it in sun or shade?
Is it wet or dry?

Many plants tolerate a range of conditions, and there are ways of improving the soil, and providing drainage and shelter. However, there is usually little that can be done about shade. Notice that there are different types of shade: permanent shade caused by buildings etc., temporary shade when the spot receives sun for only part of the day (this also depends on the time of year), and dappled shade beneath trees. Even if you can improve the conditions, the best results will always be obtained with plants that are naturally suited to your garden.

How is the garden used?
What parts do you see from the window?
Where do you sit out?
Where do children play?

It is important to provide all-year-round colour in the most visible parts of the garden, while scented flowers are most appreciated if planted by the paths or patio. A border around a makeshift football pitch or toddlers' sandpit is *not* the place for fragile, precious or poisonous plants!

How much time do you want to spend gardening?

It is possible to plan interesting and attractive areas which need very little maintenance – much less, in fact, than a lawn. On the other hand, the more demanding specialist plants can be fascinating and exciting.

How much money do you want to spend?

You can establish a flower garden at relatively little cost, particularly if you are prepared to be patient – allowing small plants to spread and doing some propagating yourself (see Chapter 3). However, it is always worth spending a little extra to get good quality plants. At a garden centre choose carefully and make sure the plants are healthy and labelled correctly. A mail-order supplier will have a greater selection but they will usually cost more.

Questions to ask about each plant

What type of soil does it need?
How hardy is it?
Does it like sun or shade?
Does it need moist or dry conditions?

You must make sure you have a suitable place to put your plants *before* you buy them. There are a few which only grow in acid soils, so watch out for these. Some others do best in limy soils. Those that are not reliably hardy may need a sheltered position if they are to survive the winter. Many do best in a soil which retains some moisture, but this does not mean they will withstand waterlogging – only a few will tolerate such conditions. Similarly, only a few will grow well in permanent shade, although many like partial and/or dappled shade: the best guide is to observe where plants are thriving in other gardens.

What colour is it?
When does it flower?
What is the foliage like?

With careful choice of plants, you can have continuous colour in your garden all year round. In a small garden it is especially important to choose plants that provide a lasting display, and that still look attractive when the flowers are over.

Is it scented?
When does it smell?

Scent is most appreciated in plants next to the paths, on a terrace, or around a garden seat, and raised beds will bring small flowers nearer 'nose level'! However, remember that some flowers only give off their scent in the evening (when they open to attract the night-flying moths in their native countries). Scent is often a quality lost when breeding highly developed garden flowers.

How tall is it?
Does it spread rapidly?
Does it need staking?

Obviously tall plants are not suitable for very small gardens, narrow beds or windy places. And staking them takes time. It is worth growing sturdy types where possible, and new dwarf varieties of common plants. But remember that height and vigour will vary with the soil and climate: measurements in catalogues are only a guide.

Does it attract wildlife to the garden?

Bees and butterflies are a pleasure to watch on a still summer's day, and bees will help pollinate fruit and vegetable crops. Some flowers also encourage beneficial insects like hoverflies whose larvae feed on aphid pests. In general, it is the single varieties of colourful and perfumed plants which these insects find most attractive for nectar and pollen. Native plants or nearly related garden varieties give the most support to other insects. Seed pods and berries are valuable for birds.

Is it resistant to pest and disease attack?

In a garden which provides well for all wildlife, pest and disease attacks rarely reach 'epidemic' proportions. However, it helps to choose plants which are likely to have least troubles. Often, highly developed and selected strains are more susceptible than their natural counterparts, but sometimes modern varieties are bred for disease resistance.

Is it good for cutting?

Flowers that can be picked and brought into the house give added pleasure, particularly in autumn and early spring when the days are short. Those that can be dried for decorative arrangements or to add to a scented 'pot-pourri' mixture extend this even to dark winter days. Some flowers are edible and can be picked to decorate salads and sweets.

Naming flowers
It is worth becoming familiar with the Latin names of plants. They may seem awkward to use at first, but many have already become common names – like

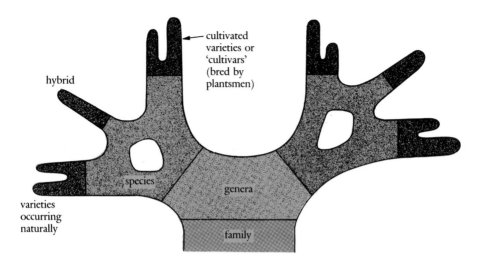

Figure 1. Botanical grouping of plants.

dahlia, chrysanthemum and clematis – and most others are no stranger to pronounce than these. Latin names should be printed in italics.

Also worth trying to understand are the botanical groupings into which plants are placed. They are first divided into loosely related 'families', then subdivided into closer 'genera' (singular 'genus') and from there into species (Figure 1). The first part of a plant's Latin name gives its genus and the second its species. For example *Tagetes erecta* (African Marigold) and *Tagetes patula* (French marigold) are both species belonging to the genus *Tagetes*.

Sometimes the species are subdivided into cultivated varieties or 'cultivars'. The cultivar name is printed in plain type inside quotation marks after the Latin: *Tagetes erecta* 'Spun Gold', for example. A third *Latin* part to the name means that the variety is naturally occurring. A multiplication sign indi-

cates that the plant is a 'hybrid' resulting from interbreeding, usually between two species of the same genus.

All this is important to the gardener because many garden plants have no common names, while others have more than one! Solomon's Seal, and David's Harp, for example, are both names for *Polygatum multiflorum* – which name you learn depends on where you live and the books you read. Sometimes the same common name is given to different plants: *Calendula* and *Tagetes* are both called 'marigolds', although they are as different from each other as either is from a daisy.

The Latin name should leave no room for mistaken identity – and this is very necessary if, for example, you are ordering by post from a seed catalogue or a nursery. It can also be usefully descriptive – perhaps of the plant's colour, form or habit – for example *Chrysanthemum 'maximum'* is the 'large' ox-eye daisy. Sometimes the name alludes to the plant's history.

Thus Latin names can be equally as fascinating as common names, and there are several books on the subject for those wishing to pursue the subject further. In this book, common names are used in the text where these are familiar and unmistakable. The Latin equivalents are given when the plant is first mentioned and in the tables and index.

CHAPTER 2

PREPARATION AND CARE OF THE FLOWER GARDEN

In organic gardening, the plants are regarded as part of a system which also includes the soil and all living organisms in the garden. You cannot look after one part of this system properly without considering the rest.

The soil

The composition of the soil is one of the first things to investigate when planning your garden. It can be anything from light, well-drained sand to very heavy clay. But, hopefully, it will be something between the two!

Improving the soil structure

You cannot change whether your soil is sandy or clay, but you can improve its properties by adding organic matter: well-rotted manure, garden compost or leaf-mould. This will help sandy soils to hold water and nutrients, and help clay soils to become more workable and drain more easily. There are some plants which can tolerate drought, and a few which do not mind 'wet feet', so it is worth seeking these out for bad sites. But in general, flowers do best on the 'moisture retentive but well-drained soil' mentioned so often in catalogue descriptions, and it is only the addition of organic matter that will produce this.

In preparing a new site, organic matter can be added to the soil by double digging (Figure 2); this also breaks up the subsoil and should help improve drainage. After planting, and in subsequent years, you can 'mulch' the plants with organic matter: that is, spread a layer of good garden compost, leaf mould, well-rotted manure, peat or composted bark on the surface of the soil around the plants. The material will gradually be worked into the soil by earthworms and hence inmprove its structure.

Mulching is also valuable for keeping moisture in the soil and for this reason should only be applied when the soil is wet: usually in the spring. You need a layer of at least 2 inches (5cm) thick to be effective – and preferably more.

The danger of organic mulches is that they can attract slugs and encourage rotting, so keep a 2–3 inches (5–7.5cm) space free around the stems of plants, especially young shoots. Peat and composted bark are the most suitable for using around bedding plants: both of these can be bought at garden centres, although it would be expensive to use them over a large area. Compost and manure are good for herbaceous plants and roses. Lawn mowings can be used here too – but spread them in a thin layer and keep them well away from the plant stems.

Soil acidity

Besides deciding what type of soil you have, you should find out how acid or alkaline it is. This can be done quite simply with a 'pH' testing kit bought from a garden shop. A pH of 7 is 'neutral'; lower values indicate acid soil and higher values alkaline soils.

There are some major groups of plants which are fussy about the pH: most heathers, azaleas and rhododendrons, for example, need an acid soil. Most flowers, however, are happy with soils of pH in the range of 6.0–7.5, although the optimum is around 6.5. Roses, lupins and lilies, for example, are said to like slightly acid soil. You may be able to tell roughly what your soil is like by observing which plants are flourishing in your neighbours' gardens.

The acidity of the soil also affects its fertility and the earthworm population: worms dislike a very acid soil. The acidity can be reduced by adding lime but only do this if you are sure it is necessary (detailed instructions are usually given with the pH testing kits). Calcified seaweed is also very good for reducing acidity and has additional benefits for the soil. It is not easy to make an alkaline soil more acid: the best method is the continual addition of organic matter – particularly peat – over successive seasons.

Fertility and plant feeding

Most flowers do not demand a lot of plant foods – in fact sometimes a rich soil can actually be a problem, encouraging leafy growth at the expense of blooms. Sandy soils are the most likely to lack fertility. Most garden soils, however, have easily enough nutrients in them to grow flowers. Problems arise not because the nutrients are lacking but because the plants cannot get at them.

First, the plant can only search out enough food if it can make a good root system, so compacted soil must be dug and the soil structure improved by adding organic matter, as described earlier. Second, if the soil is either too

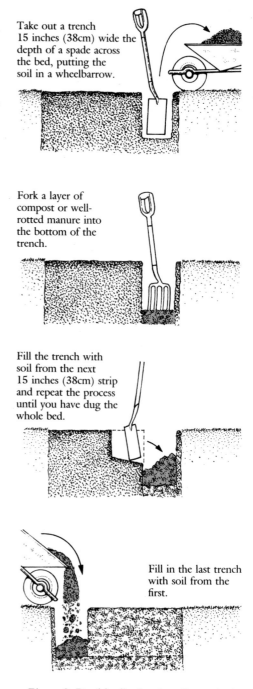

Take out a trench 15 inches (38cm) wide the depth of a spade across the bed, putting the soil in a wheelbarrow.

Fork a layer of compost or well-rotted manure into the bottom of the trench.

Fill the trench with soil from the next 15 inches (38cm) strip and repeat the process until you have dug the whole bed.

Fill in the last trench with soil from the first.

Figure 2. Double digging in a flower bed.

alkaline or too acid, certain nutrients may become either 'locked up' in the soil or washed out: this affects the general health of the plants even if they show no particular symptoms, and should be corrected as described in the previous section.

The best way to make sure plants get enough nutrients is to return waste plant material to the soil in the form of compost: forked in before planting or as a mulch around perennial plants. As well as improving the soil structure, compost provides a steady, balanced diet for the plants as it is slowly broken down by micro-organisms in the soil. It will contain a wide range of nutrients – not just the two or three provided by chemical fertilizers. Deep-rooted garden plants and weeds are especially valuable in taking up minerals from the soil; when these go into the compost, they become available to other plants.

Although leaf-mould and peat are good soil conditioners, they contain few nutrients; forest bark may actually deplete the soil of nitrogen and hence should be used with an organic fertilizer like fishmeal, as described later. To feed demanding plants like dahlias or to improve a poor soil, use additional quantities of well-rotted manure.

Making garden compost and leaf-mould
Any pile of vegetable waste will decay – eventually. Making compost just means helping the natural process of decay along a bit. The simplest method of doing this is to pile up a big heap of moist material – at least 3 feet (1 m) each way – and cover it with black polythene. This will be ready to use in about a year, but it will not be as good as compost made more carefully and quickly in proper bins. Fine, crumbly compost can be produced in two or three months in bins, and heat generated in the process will kill weed seeds,

pests and disease organisms.

Bins should be made of an insulating material such as breeze blocks, bricks or wood. They should measure about 3 feet (1 m) each way (Figure 3). Smaller bins do not make compost efficiently because a lot of the material touches the walls and gets cold and dry. This is the main problem with most ready-made bins available in the shops so it is well worth your while making your own.

The bacteria which bring about the quick decay need moisture, warmth and air. They also need a good mixture of stemmy or strawy materials (which provide carbon) and leafy materials or grass (which provide nitrogen) on which to work. Thus you should avoid putting a solid mass of any one substance on the heap: mix your mowings with tough weeds or old straw, for example. In winter you may need to add nitrogen in the form of chicken manure, dried blood or fishmeal.

For the best and quickest results, build two – or even three – bins together so that you can turn the heap from one to the other. This is best done about a week after building the heap – and again a few weeks later if you can! It aerates the material, keeps the bacteria active, and causes the temperature of the heap to rise. If you are not confident of creating such a 'hot' heap, you would be wise to exclude the roots of perennial weeds like couch grass from your compost material.

Some leaves can go on the compost heap, but if you have a lot it is best to treat them separately. Pile them inside a wire-netting frame, treading them down as you go, and leave them to decompose slowly. After about two years they will have turned into dark fibrous 'leaf-mould' which is pleasant to handle and very useful in the garden.

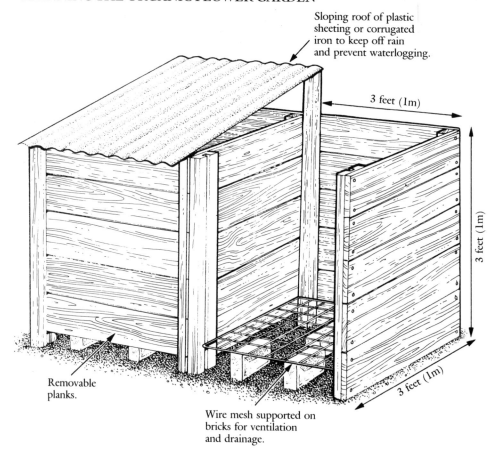

Sloping roof of plastic sheeting or corrugated iron to keep off rain and prevent waterlogging.

3 feet (1m)

3 feet (1m)

Removable planks.

Wire mesh supported on bricks for ventilation and drainage.

3 feet (1m)

Figure 3. A home-made wooden compost bin.

Organic fertilizers

The practice of automatically adding general chemical fertilizers to flower beds is at the very least a waste of money, and can be positively harmful: the nitrogen they contain is taken straight up by the plant causing sappy growth – much loved by aphids. Plants overfed with the main chemical elements may also be unable to take up from the soil the minor elements which they need: small amounts of these are essential to their health. Meanwhile the soil micro-organisms are dulled into inactivity.

In some cases, however, the addition of a little 'organic' fertilizer can be helpful. Organic fertilizers are those of animal or vegetable origin: they are concentrated sources of plant foods, but still have to be worked on by soil micro-organisms before they can be used by the plants.

The most useful organic fertilizer in the flower garden is bonemeal. This gives a slow steady supply of phosphorus which supports strong root and flower growth; it is particularly good for plants that stay in the ground year after year: naturalized bulbs and roses, for example. Fishmeal is a more general, quicker acting organic fertilizer; it is useful on poor new soils, applied together with leaf-mould, peat or compost. Use about 2 oz per square yard (approx. 60 grams per square metre). Quick acting organic nitrogen fertilizers like dried blood are best used to activate the compost heap rather than put directly onto the flower garden.

Calcified seaweed is a useful source of all the minerals needed in small amounts by plants, and may also help the soil structure. Seaweed extract, bought as a concentrated liquid like chemical liquid feeds, contains a similar range of minerals. It makes a good 'tonic' for plants which are recovering from a pest or disease attack, or suffering from some mineral deficiency. The mixture can be watered onto the roots or sprayed directly onto the leaves; the dilution rate varies, so follow the manufacturers' instructions.

Seaweed extracts do not, however, contain the quantity of nutrients required to feed plants kept in pots for a long period. There are stronger organic feeds based on liquid manure available, but you can make an equally good one yourself from the leaves of Russian comfrey (*Symphytum* × *uplandicum*). This is a vigorous relative of the wild comfrey (*Symphytum officinalis*) and ornamental comfrey varieties (see Chapter 6): a patch of it growing in an odd corner of the garden can be cut three or four times a year. A brew is made by loosely packing the leaves in a bucket and topping it up with water. Cover the top and leave it for two to four weeks until the comfrey has fermented and turned black. The clear brown comfrey liquid can then be strained off, ready for use.

Weed control

No weedkillers are used in the organic flower garden; these are often harmful to soil organisms and wildlife as well as to you and your garden plants. It is thus essential to clear the ground of any perennial weeds before planting – and you need to start this well in advance if the site is badly infested.

Weeds with tap roots, like dandelions and docks, can be dug out; if you break them they will resprout so allow time for several attempts. Shallow-rooted weeds like couch grass and ground elder can be destroyed by continually forking or using a Rotavator and raking out the roots during a dry spell in summer, although on a poor soil this can be difficult. Bindweed and creeping thistle are two of the worst weeds: their roots can go down 18 inches (45 cm) or more and any little piece left in the ground will produce a new plant.

A good way to clear a really weedy patch is to cover it for a whole growing season with a material that the weeds cannot penetrate: black plastic (buried at the edges to hold it), a thick layer of newspaper (weighted down with stones or straw), or a piece of old carpet. Even the worst perennial weeds should have been stifled by the time the material is removed in the autumn.

After planting, keep the ground free of weeds by hoeing and hand weeding: if you do not let any new perennial weeds get a hold or allow annuals to seed, your work should lessen considerably in subsequent years. A thick mulch of organic material (as described earlier) will prevent weeds from germinating and can be a great help, but take care that you do not introduce more weed seeds in badly made compost, manure or lawn mowings.

Occasionally, black plastic can be used as a temporary weed control after planting. For example, a mat about 3 feet square (1 m square) could be placed around new shrub roses planted in rough grass; this should prevent the grass from competing with the shrub for water and nutrients during its first summer. But remember that large areas of plastic will prevent water from entering as well as leaving the soil; they are also unsightly. A layer of gravel 2 – 3 inches (5 – 7.5 cm) thick looks attractive around the base of climbing roses or on a small bed of rock plants close to the house. It will conserve much needed moisture, as well as control weeds, and will help keep the bases of rock plants clean and dry.

Pest and disease control

Chemical pesticides and fungicides cause great harm to wildlife. They also destroy the natural enemies of pests as well as their targets. As a result, survivors multiply rapidly causing even more trouble than before, and 'new' pests are created because less common insects – whose occasional nibbles were previously of little consequence – increase in numbers. It is far better to tolerate some damage and let a natural balance establish itself between friend and foe in the garden.

Avoiding attacks

There are, however, several things you can do to help tip that balance in your favour. First, inspect any bought plants carefully, and be sure not to introduce any pests or diseases into the garden. Try to avoid types that are particularly prone to pest and disease attack: this still gives you a very wide choice as the following chapters will show! There may be resistant varieties even within groups of plants that are normally susceptible: for example, the aster *Aster frikarti* rarely suffers from the powdery mildew which bedevils so many Michaelmas daisies. (Many other examples are given in the pest and diseases sections in Chapters 4 – 7.)

However, *any* plant's best defence against pests and diseases is health and vigour, and flowers grown organically are far more able to withstand attack. Choose those that like the conditions in your garden rather than those that will have to struggle against them, and prepare the ground thoroughly.

You can also help decrease the numbers of pests in your garden by encouraging their natural predators. Hoverflies, for example, will gather to feed on flowers that are flat and open in shape, like poached-egg flowers (*Limnanthes*), marigolds (*Calendula*), rudbeckia and yarrow (*Achillea*). Most hoverflies will then seek out aphid-infested plants on which to lay their eggs, and the larvae that hatch will consume a significant number of the pests. Ladybirds and ladybird larvae also eat aphids, so take care not to burn dry vegetation in which the adults are hibernating. Growing a good mixture of plant species – especially of the old cottage garden flowers which are similar in form to native plants – will generally encourage a good pest–predator balance.

Many birds are good predators – although they can, of course, be pests too! Tits eat many small insect pests, and blackbirds and thrushes eat slugs. Starlings are said to be especially fond of millepedes. Hedgehogs, toads and frogs all feed on slugs' eggs and young slugs. So, encourage these creatures wherever possible and do not put their lives in danger by poisoning slugs with chemical baits.

Physical methods of control

Once your plants are growing well, keep a close watch for trouble and try to identify any symptoms quickly. Attacks can often be stemmed by simple physical means if you catch them in time: caterpillars can be picked off by hand, leaf miners squashed and diseased leaves removed and burnt. If a plant suddenly dies, dig it up and look at the roots to see if you can see any root pests.

Dry leaves and other debris can harbour both pests and predators, so tidiness in the garden will always be a compromise. However, never leave diseased foliage or dead plants lying around the garden to infect others. Many disease spores and pests are destroyed in the heat of a *good* compost heap, but if you are unsure it is better to burn infected material. Rotting vegetation will also attract slugs.

Trapping is another physical method of pest control. You may be able to tempt millepedes and wireworms away from your new lily bulbs by burying small mesh bags of potato peelings nearby; empty and burn the contents at least every week. Slug traps can be set up by sinking saucers in the ground and filling them with a sweet liquid – beer is said to be the best! The slugs are attracted in, but cannot climb out. If you empty and refill these traps regularly, you should be able to reduce significantly the numbers of slugs in the garden. However, there is no guarantee that survivors will not still prefer your young bedding plants or new lily shoots. Small numbers of plants can be protected by individual 'open cloches' made from plastic lemonade bottles. For larger beds, a thin mulch of dry peat or other scratchy material can help, since slugs prefer moist conditions and dislike putting themselves at risk of drying out (Figure 4).

Organic pesticides and fungicides
If – and only if – a pest or disease attack cannot be dealt with in any other way, there are 'organic' sprays that can be used: these are of vegetable origin and hence break down quickly in the soil into natural harmless products. Used

Protection for individual plants using a tubular section cut from a clear plastic drinks bottle.

Figure 4. A way of combating slugs.

properly, they have least effect on the wildlife that you want to encourage: the butterflies, bees and the enemies of pests and disease organisms.

Derris (made from the root of a tropical plant) is one of the most useful pesticides and is easy to obtain as either a liquid or dust. It is effective against small caterpillars, aphids and flea beetle, but is also harmful to bees, so always spray flowers in the late evening.

Pyrethrum (made from a type of chrysanthemum native to Kenya) can be used in a similar way. It is not so widely available, however, and some formulations contain synthetic pyrethroids which should not be used.

Quassia (from the bark of a tropical tree) will kill aphids, small caterpillars and some mites. It is sometimes sold as chips which have to be simmered in water. The liquid is most effective if soap flakes (or even a few drops of washing-up liquid) are added, and, in fact, soapy water alone is of some use against aphids.

Bacillus thuringiensis – marketed under several trade names – is a caterpillar spray of a different nature. It is a 'biological' spray containing the spores of bacteria which are activated in the caterpillar's gut and prevent it feeding. It will kill most small caterpillars – although some large ones may be less affected – and it is completely safe for all other life in the garden.

There are no organic off-the-shelf fungicides easily obtainable, but a home-made preparation from elder leaves is worth trying against some fungal diseases. Simmer about 1 lb (454 g) of leaves in 6 pints (3.4 l) of water for half an hour, strain it and use it undiluted.

Identification of pests and diseases
Tables 1 and 2 should help you identify most of the common pests and diseases found in the garden. This is particularly important to the organic gardener. For example, you need to resist the temptation to stamp on any ugly-looking insect, as it might be a useful predator. Knowing something about the life of the pest or disease organism is also useful: it makes you realize which good garden practices prevent problems occurring.

Although the tables are long, you would be unlucky if more than a few of the pests or diseases listed became a problem in any one year. In most gardens, unhealthy plants are more likely to result from other factors – poor feeding, bad drainage, over-shading, cold, wrong soil type – and this should not happen in the well-planned organic garden!

Table 1: Identification and control of flower pests.

Pest	Description	Symptoms	Avoidance and control measures
Aphids	Small winged insects: pear-shaped bodies usually about 0.1 inch (2mm) long, transparent wings. Common types affecting flowers: blackfly, greenfly (rose-aphid), peach-potato aphid (buff coloured), lupin aphid (light green and much larger).	Occur on leaves, young shoots and flower buds where they suck sap, causing weakening and distortion. Exude a sticky 'honeydew' on which a sooty mould may form. Transmit virus diseases.	Encourage natural predators such as hoverflies, ladybirds and lacewings. Spray with derris, pyrethrum, quassia or soft soap.
Capsid bugs	Oval green bugs about 0.2 inch (5mm) long.	Suck sap, causing distortion and small ragged holes in leaves; attack a wide range of plants. Not all similar bugs are harmful, so identification is important.	Hand-picking – difficult to control with sprays.
Caterpillars of moths and butterflies (see also cutworms and swift moth)	No black markings on legs. A few that feed on ornamental plants are those of mullein moths (yellow and black), buff-tip moth (yellow and black), orange-tip butterfly.	Eat holes in leaves but numbers are not usually great. Most caterpillars do not eat garden plants, so only destroy them if they are 'caught in the act'; even then you may prefer to have the butterflies.	Hand-picking is best for a few. If more numerous, spray with derris or biological spray.
Chafers	Beetles and larvae cause damage. Cockchafer adult – brown, 1 inch (2.5cm), larvae – fat, white 1.5 inch (4cm). The larvae of the other chafers are similar but smaller.	Adult garden chafers chew holes in leaves of many plants and the rose chafer feeds on the leaves and blooms of roses and other large flowers. Commonest in May and June. Larvae in soil feed on bulbs and roots and may cause plants suddenly to wilt and die.	Damage by adults is seldom severe – control by hand-picking. Larvae can be harmful – their numbers can be reduced by deep cultivation whenever appropriate, exposing them to birds and other predators.

Pest	Description	Symptoms	Avoidance and control measures
	Garden chafer adult – green and brown 0.6 inch (15mm).		
	Summer chafer adult – orangey brown 0.6 inch (15mm). Rose chafer adult – green 0.6 inch (15mm).		
Cutworms	Fat dirty green or grey brown caterpillars about 1 inch (2.5cm) long; the larvae of several types of moth, most commonly the turnip moth, the heart and dart moth and the large yellow underwing.	Feed mainly on roots and stems of many garden plants and weeds, often severing them at soil level (hence their name).	Numbers reduced by frequent cultivation and weeding. The open 'cloches' used for slugs give some protection to individual young plants.
Earwigs	Several species may be in the garden, but all have unmistakable pincers at their tail.	Hide inside flowers, particularly full ones such as carnations, and eat ragged holes in the petals and leaves.	Trap them in inverted flower pots loosely filled with newspaper or dry straw, emptied daily.
Eelworms	Tiny thin roundworms – often not visible to the naked eye. Eggs are deposited in a tough 'cyst'.	Live within tissues of susceptible plants, damaging the roots and causing stunting, discoloration and wilting. Can badly affect some herbaceous plants (e.g., phlox) – and bulbs (particularly narcissi – brown rings visible if bulb is cut open).	Destroy infested plants and avoid replanting susceptible hosts for at least three years – a few eelworm cysts can survive up to ten years in the soil without hatching.
Flea beetles	Dark shiny beetles only about 0.3 inch (7mm) long which leap away when disturbed.	Eat small circular holes in leaves of plants in the brassica family such as alyssum, stocks and wallflowers. They are most active in hot dry weather and can severely damage seedlings.	Watering and good growing conditions to help plants grow away can be sufficient. Otherwise dust or spray with derris: clear away dead leaves and other debris where beetles overwinter.

Pest	Description	Symptoms	Avoidance and control measures
Froghoppers	Brown leaping frog-like bugs about 0.25 inch (6mm) long. Produce the familiar dollops of froth or 'cuckoo spit' on ornamental plants.	Feed on plant sap and can distort young growth, but rarely seen in sufficient numbers to cause much damage.	Take off by hand or with a jet of water.
Leafhoppers	Aphid-like insects which spring off plants when disturbed.	Suck sap and cause mottling of leaves of a wide range of plants – often noticeable on roses. Damage is generally slight, but they may spread virus disease.	Spray bad infestations as for aphids.
Leafminers	Tiny insects which live in spaces between the upper and lower surfaces of leaves – they are the larvae of various species of moths and flies.	Causes 'mines' in leaves – winding tunnels or blotches clearly visible. Different species attack different plants but aqualegias and chrysanthemums are commonly affected.	Remove and destroy infested leaves as soon as possible.
Leatherjackets (crane-fly larvae)	Fat legless grey-brown grubs about 0.75 inch (2cm) long living in the soil.	Feed on plant roots causing wilting, and will surface and nibble stems on wet nights. Numerous in grassland and neglected sites, so tend to be troublesome when these are first cultivated.	Reduce numbers by frequent deep cultivation where appropriate. Can be brought to the surface by soaking the area with water and covering overnight with black polythene.

Pest	Description	Symptoms	Avoidance and control measures
Millepedes	There are two common harmful garden millepedes: the black millepede which has a shiny tough cylindrical body and coils up when disturbed, and the spotted snake millepede which has a light brown body with a row of red spots along each side.	Feed on plant roots, bulbs and tubers, chiefly if they are already damaged; attacks may be worse in drought conditions.	Numbers reduced by deep cultivation where appropriate and by trapping (see text). Avoid damage to roots and bulbs.
Narcissus fly larvae	Short fat maggots which tunnel into bulbs.	Infected bulbs go soft in store; in the ground they die or produce a few stunted leaves and no flowers. Daffodils are most commonly affected although snowdrops, snowflakes and others can be.	Discard soft bulbs at lifting or planting. Hoe well after flowering to prevent the fly from laying its eggs in holes in soil left by dying leaves.
Pea and bean weevils	Small 0.25 inch (6mm) dark beetles with a prolonged 'snout'. Larvae are white legless grubs.	Adults eat scalloped shaped holes in the edges of sweet pea leaves; larvae feed on roots. Damage is worse on seedlings in April and May.	Spray or dust seedlings with derris. Raise plants inside in pots. Mature plants should withstand attacks.
Red spider mite	Tiny pale orange globular creatures about 0.04 inch (1mm) long.	Suck sap and cause light mottling of leaves of roses and sometimes herbaceous plants.	Natural predators should keep these in check. Spray with derris if necessary.
Sawfly larvae	Most resemble small butterfly caterpillars, but have more rear legs. Species vary in colour and markings.	Many species feed on leaves, like caterpillars, and can cause severe damage on some plants; e.g., Solomon's seal. Others feed inside tissues and cause galls. Rose leaf-curling sawfly rolls up the leaves.	Spray surface-feeding larvae with derris. Others can only be controlled by removing and burning affected leaves.

Pest	Description	Symptoms	Avoidance and control measures
Slugworms	A species of sawfly larvae which look more like slugs than caterpillars. Dirty green, 0.5 inch (12mm) long.	Scrape upper green surface of rose leaves, leaving transparent patches.	Remove by hand or spray with derris.
Slugs and snails	The most harmful are the netted slug (small, fawn and white), the garden slug (dark with a yellow sole) and the underground keeled slugs (black or brown).	The netted and garden slugs eat any green leaves, with an especial liking for seedlings and young shoots. The underground keeled slugs damage roots, tubers etc.	Trap with saucers of beer to reduce numbers; protect plants with open 'cloches' (see Figure 4) or a mulch of dry material. Remove rotting plant debris.
Swift moth larvae	Dirty white caterpillars 1–2 inches (2.5–5.0cm) long with brown heads; live in the soil.	Feed on roots and bulbs of many cultivated plants and weeds.	Good weed control helps, since moths rarely lay eggs on bare soil. Frequent cultivation, where appropriate, will reduce numbers.
Thrips (thunderflies)	Tiny, slender black insects, usually less than 0.1 inch (2mm) long; winged species take flight in sultry weather.	Suck sap of leaves and flowers; results in silver streaks on leaves; flowers mottled with withered edges; sometimes distortion.	Spray with derris.
Vine weevil larvae	Small white grubs about 0.15 inch (4mm) long.	Eat plant roots; most troublesome in potted plants, but can cause damage in the garden.	Frequent cultivation outdoors; use sterilized potting compost where possible.
Wireworms (click beetle larvae)	Tough yellow-brown cylindrical bodies ½–1 inch (13–25mm) long with three pairs of legs; live in the soil.	Feed on plant roots, bulbs and tubers, especially dahlias and gladioli.	Usually only numerous on a new site; reduce numbers by frequent cultivation and trapping.

Table 2: Identification and control of flower diseases.

Disease	Symptoms	Plants affected	Control
Blackspot (see also leaf spots)	Round black spots with fringed edges, appear on leaves in midsummer.	Modern bush roses and some modern climbing roses.	Avoid planting in closed-in spots. Clear away dead leaves in autumn. Spray with elder-leaf fungicide.
Botrytis (grey mould)	Fluffy grey mould which can affect leaves, stems and flowers.	All types of plant. Bedding plants, and peonies are particularly susceptible.	Avoid damp, crowded conditions. Remove and burn infected parts as soon as possible.
Bulb rots (see also narcissus smoulder and tulip fire)	Several fungi and bacteria cause mushy rotten bulbs: a brown basal rot and a grey rot are common. Yellow stunted shoots may be produced in early stages. White rot covers bulbs with a fluffy fungal growth.	Basal rot: mainly lilies and daffodils. Grey rot: mainly tulips and hyacinths but also other common bulbs. White rot affects alliums.	Do not plant in badly drained soil. Dig up and destroy infected plants. Inspect bought bulbs carefully. Do not replant alliums on infected soil.
Clubroot	Swollen, distorted roots; stunted plants.	Cruciferous plants: wallflowers, stocks.	Lime acid soils. Avoid planting susceptible species (clubroot spores can last up to twenty years in the soil).
Corm rots	Various types of rot include a soft rot affecting stored corms, a dry rot, and a hard rot which causes shrivelling.	Mainly gladioli, but also crocus and other corms.	Destroy diseased plants – do not leave infected debris in soil. Inspect bought bulbs carefully.
Die back	Tip of a branch becomes unhealthy and dies; the process may continue back down branch.	All types of roses.	Cut infected shoots back to living tissue. Check growing conditions (see Chapter 7).
Downy mildew	White tufty mould, usually on undersides of leaves. Less commonly seen than powdery mildew or botrytis.	Can affect any plants – particularly young ones – but sweet peas, and antirrhinums may be susceptible.	Avoid overcrowded damp conditions. Remove and destroy infected leaves.
Foot rot	Fungus causing blackening and rotting of the base of stems.	Commonly seen on annual asters, petunias, pansies and campanula.	Avoid waterlogging and remove all plant debris. Do not grow susceptible plants again in the same soil.

Disease	Symptoms	Plants affected	Control
Leaf spots	Many different fungi and bacteria cause spots on leaves – each usually specific to a particular plant. The spot can take the form of dark rounds or ovals, blotches or concentric rings.	Can affect any plants but damage is not usually serious, two exceptions being roses (*see* Blackspot) and hellebores.	Remove infected leaves, and winter leaf debris; try elder spray in bad cases.
Narcissus smoulder	Decaying shoots; rotting bulbs.	Narcissi.	Discard soft bulbs before planting. Dig up and destroy badly affected plants.
Powdery mildew	White powdery coating on stems and leaves.	A wide range of plants; delphiniums, chrysanthemums, Michaelmas daisies and roses often affected.	Avoid dry, overcrowded conditions: watering and mulching helps. Try elder spray in bad cases or grow resistant varieties.
Rhizome rot	Leaf tips yellow and wither. A soft rot affects the rhizomes.	Irises.	Make sure site is properly drained. Avoid bruising rhizomes. Destroy infected plants.
Rust	Orange or brown spots on leaves and stems caused by several different fungi.	Common on: antirrhinums, chrysanthemums, hollyhocks, roses and sweet williams. Some rust fungi can spread from one type of plant to another; others are specific to just one.	Can be difficult to control. Plants underfed and underwatered are more susceptible. Grow resistant varieties where available and raise new plants of hollyhocks and antirrhinums annually. Burn diseased leaves – particularly at the end of the season to destroy overwintering spores, although some rusts are contained within the plant tissues.

Disease	Symptoms	Plants affected	Control
Tuber rots	Soft fungal rots can destroy tubers in storage.	All tubers.	Inspect bought tubers carefully.
Tulip fire	Scorched areas on leaves, spots on flowers, fungal rotting of bulb.	Tulips.	Worse in cold, wet conditions. Check bulbs before planting and destroy all infected plants.
Virus diseases	Many different symptoms but common ones include: mottled yellow or brown patches on leaves; stunted growth; distorted leaves and/or flowers; flower colour streaky or patchy.	Any plant.	There is no cure. Remove and burn infected plants. Buy plants from reputable source and use only healthy plants for propagation. Keep plants free from aphids and other sap-sucking insects which spread the diseases.
Wilt	A soil-borne fungus causing plants to wilt even though the soil is moist.	Particularly antirrhinums, asters, carnations, lupins and sweet peas.	Remove diseased plants. Do not grow the same plants on the same spot every year.

CHAPTER 3
PROPAGATING YOUR OWN PLANTS

Propagating your own plants can undoubtedly save you money – and it can be fun and rewarding too. You can afford to plant more lavishly and experiment with the unfamiliar.

Annuals and biennials must be propagated from seed, and this method can be used for many herbaceous perennials and some bulbs, corms and tubers with good results. However, sometimes it takes several years for a perennial seedling to reach flowering size and the quality of the plants obtained can be variable. This last problem can be overcome by 'vegetative' propagation, using pieces taken from a single parent plant. The new plants will be identical to the parent: in colour, pattern and height, for example.

Sowing seeds
The main conditions needed for good seed germination are warmth and moisture, and most seeds will grow well if you ensure that these are met. However, the seeds of some perennials have additional requirements. Delphinium seeds, for example, are more likely to be successful if they are really fresh. Those of some hellebores need to have experienced frosty conditions before they will germinate: you must sow them in autumn or give them an artificial winter in the fridge! Sweet peas (*Lathyrus*) and lupins (*Lupinus*) have a hard seed coat, and chipping this with a knife or gently rubbing it with sandpaper will help

germination. Other problems may be simply that seeds are very small, or that they germinate erratically over a long period. The instructions in this chapter and in the last sections of Chapters 4 – 6 should help you overcome these. In contrast, some hardy annuals and biennials germinate almost too easily and self-sown seedlings will appear all over the garden. Some perennials like aqualegias and astrantia will also readily self-seed.

Sowing seeds in the garden
Hardy annuals are sown directly where they are to flower in the garden; biennials and some perennials are often sown in rows in a separate 'nursery' seed bed. In either case, good preparation of the bed is essential. Fork it to loosen any compaction and then rake until the soil particles are like fine crumbs. This will be easy if the soil is damp – but not so wet that it sticks to your shoes – and you should try to catch it like this for sowing your seeds.

Sow in rows by making a shallow drill with a hoe or a trowel to the recommended depth. This will depend on the size of the seed and your type of soil: the bigger the seed and the lighter your soil, the deeper it should be. Sow the seed *thinly* and cover the drill gently with soil. Never water *after* sowing: this packs down the soil and can cause a hard crust or 'cap' to form when it dries out. If you have to sow into dry soil, trickle water along the bottom of the drill before you put in the seeds. If you have to sow in wet conditions, use peat rather than sticky soil to cover the drills. This also helps if the soil is lumpy or prone to capping after rain.

When the seedlings emerge they will need careful hand-weeding. Thin them to about 2 inches (5cm) apart at first; later, thin annuals to their final spacing and biennials and perennials to about 6 inches (15cm) – judge it so that the seedlings are never in competition with one another.

Sowing seeds in pots

This method is used for half-hardy annuals which need a warm start indoors to bring them on to flowering size. It is also more reliable for small numbers of perennials and biennials: especially appropriate if seed is expensive or slow to germinate.

The problem in raising your own plants organically is that nearly all the seed and potting 'composts' on the market contain chemicals. So you may have to compromise by buying a proprietary soil-based mix (where at

Table 3: Possible sowing and potting mixtures. (All quantities are approximate because organic fertilizers and manures are variable.)

Sowing compost	Comment
1. Proprietary soil-based (John Innes) compost.	Contains chemicals.
2. Peat plus horticultural sand (1:1 ratio by volume). Soak peat in liquid seaweed or add 1 ounce (28g) of calcified seaweed/2 gallon bucketful.	Seedlings must be pricked out into a potting mixture (which contains more nutrients) at an early stage.
3. Peat + hort. sand + mushroom compost (2:1:1)	Mushroom compost often contains residue of chemicals.
Peat + hort. sand + worm compost (2:1:1) + 1 ounce (28g) calcified seaweed or lime/2 gallon bucketful.	Worm compost can be bought, but is not widely available.
Peat + hort. sand + sterilized soil (2:1:3) + 1 ounce (28g) calcified seaweed or lime/2 gallon bucketful.	Sterilizing soil in your kitchen can be messy! Putting it in the oven can bake it too much. The best method is to steam it in a saucepan.
Potting compost for young plants	
1. Proprietary soil-based (John Innes No. 1) compost.	Contains chemicals.
2. Good soil + peat + hort. sand (8:3:1) + 4 ounces (113g) fish, blood and bone + ¾ ounce (21g) wood ash in a 2 gallon bucketful.	It is not so important to have sterilized soil here: soil from molehills or from deciduous woods is often good.
3. Good soil + peat + hort. sand (8:3:1) + 4 ounces (113g) dried manure + ¾ ounce (21g) wood ash in a 2 gallon bucketful.	Proprietary brands of dried animal and poultry manures are quite widely available. May contain chemicals.
Potting compost for large tubs of bedding plants, etc.	
Good soil + peat + garden compost/well rotted manure (5:4:2) + fertilizer (as above).	Mixture not so critical, but the addition of some materials such as peat and compost to prevent the soil packing down is essential.

1. Primroses and pasque flowers – both native plants – give a good early spring display in the garden.

2. Traditional bedding with a difference – naturalized dwarf tulips and forget-me-nots bloom in April.

3. Snake's-head fritillaries bloom in May alongside late daffodils in summer-mown grass.

(a)   (b)

4. Alliums: (a) in flower in early summer; (b) seedhead used dried in winter flower arrangements.

5. The poached-egg plant (*Limnanthes douglasii*) is one of the best for attracting hoverflies.

6. Spires of self-sown foxgloves in a cottage garden.

least some of the nutrients come from the soil) or experiment with some of the DIY mixtures suggested in Table 3. It is important that any mixture used in a pot has a good structure so that it retains moisture and does not pack down hard. Seed sowing mixtures should also be sterile. Ordinary garden soil on its own is *not* suitable. Tiny seedlings do not need much in the way of plant foods – and in fact using a rich mixture for seedlings can damage them. However, they must either be transferred to a potting compost or watered with a liquid fertilizer when they get larger.

The technique of sowing the seeds is illustrated in Figure 5. You can sow lots of seed in one pot and 'prick out' the seedlings, which makes best use of limited space in a propagator or other warm spot. Alternatively, you can sow directly into individual pots or divided polystyrene trays, so that the seedlings are not shocked by transplanting.

Cover the pots with glass or plastic to keep them moist and put them somewhere warm to germinate. A temperature of about 15–20°C is recommended for many half-hardy annuals, which means using a heated propagator or a warm spot in the house – perhaps even the airing cupboard. For perennials and biennials sown later in the year, temperatures in an unheated greenhouse or even outside are often suitable. In either case, shield them from sunlight. As soon as the germinating seedlings are visible, move the pots or trays into a good light (although still not direct sunlight at first).

Seedlings grown in one pot must be transferred into trays or individual pots containing a weak potting mixture as soon as they are large enough to handle – usually when their first true leaves have grown. With seeds sown in individual pots, remove the weakest

Fill pots loosely to the brim with sowing compost, then firm this to give a smooth surface.

½ inch gap (12mm)

Space large seeds out over the surface about ½ inch (12mm) apart. With very fine seeds such as lobelia, tap them off the edge of a knife blade.

Cover large seeds lightly with coarsely sieved compost. Very fine seeds should not be covered.

Stand pots in a water bath until the surface is wet, then remove them and allow excess water to drain away.

Figure 5. Seed sowing in pots.

seedlings and let the strongest grow on. These may need watering with a liquid feed before they are ready for planting out.

Division of herbaceous perennials

This practice is used not only to propagate new perennials but also to keep established clumps of plants healthy and under control. The best time to divide most plants is during a moist, mild spell in late autumn or early spring; the leaves have been cut back and the plants are partly dormant so they will concentrate on establishing good roots. However, clumps of spring flowering perennials such as primulas should be left until early summer, and may need regular watering to help them re-establish themselves.

The method used to split a particular plant depends on the nature of its growth. Large clumps of loose-rooted perennials such as Michaelmas daisies can be prised apart with two forks placed back to back (Figure 6). On good soil, small plants such as primulas can be dug up and pulled apart by hand. You may have to resort to slicing plants that have solid crowns with a spade: day lilies (*Hemerocallis*), for example.

In all cases, keep only vigorous pieces

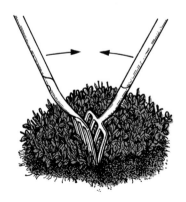

Figure 6. Dividing herbaceous perennials.

from the outside of the clump for replanting, and discard those at the centre which are likely to be under-nourished and weak. If you are re-establishing the old clump in its original position, take the opportunity to dig some well-rotted compost into the spot before replanting three or four new pieces.

New plants from bulbs and corms

Many bulbs grow to a certain size and then divide to produce two or three smaller bulbs or 'offsets' – you can often buy daffodil bulbs that have begun this process (Figure 7a). Other bulbs do not divide but produce smaller bulbs or 'bulblets' round the parent bulb. You can increase your stock by digging up the bulbs and detaching any offsets or bulblets that break away easily. It is often a good idea to grow them on in a nursery bed for one or two years until they reach flowering size. Corms, such as crocuses, produce tiny 'cormlets' which can similarly be used to produce new flowering plants in about three years (Figure 7b).

Clumps of naturalized bulbs and corms should be lifted and divided in this way every four or five years, otherwise they tend to become crowded and produce smaller flowers. A mixture of parent bulbs and offsets or bulblets can be planted over a wider area and left to re-establish.

New plants from tubers and rhizomes

Tubers can be multiplied by cutting them into pieces, each of which must contain at least one 'eye', which is the bud from which new shoots grow. You can often see the new buds clearly in spring, which is the best time for this operation.

Irises with rhizomes on the surface should be divided soon after flowering.

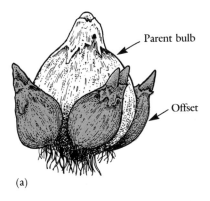

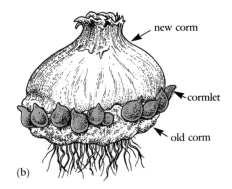

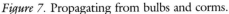

Figure 7. Propagating from bulbs and corms.

Trim back the leaves and cut them so each piece has both leaves and roots (Figure 8). Underground rhizomes are easy to pull apart when lifted; again, each new portion should have a shoot.

Soft-stem cuttings

New shoots can often be induced to produce roots of their own, and this gives a method of creating new plants without the disturbance to the parent plant that division causes. It works well for herbaceous perennials like Michaelmas daisies, pinks (*Dianthus*) and phlox.

The best time for taking cuttings is spring or early autumn. Choose young shoots with leaves closely spaced on the stem (never those with flower buds). The cuttings should be 2–4 inches (5–10cm) long. Those which root most easily are 'basal' cuttings, pulled off from the crown of the plant, or side shoots pulled from the main stem with a 'heel' of old growth visible; alternatively cut the tip of a larger shoot immediately below a leaf joint (Figure 9).

The cuttings should be inserted into pots of a peat/sand mixture as shown in Figure 10. They must now be kept moist and warm until they have rooted. A propagator with a heated floor to encourage rooting and a plastic cover to maintain humidity is ideal for this, but most will root without such lavish treatment. A good alternative is to cover each pot loosely with a polythene bag and stand it on a tray of moist sand in a warm, light (but not sunny) position. In summer, many herbaceous

Figure 8. Dividing an iris rhizome.

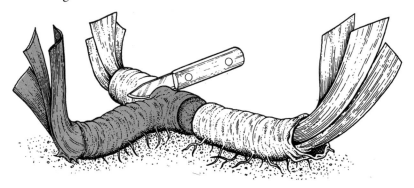

perennials will root simply in a shaded cold frame. They should not need the help of hormone rooting powders (which contain a chemical fungicide): calcified seaweed, added to the compost in the pot, is said to aid rooting.

When you see the first signs of new growth on the cuttings, bring the pots gradually into normal sunny airy conditions. Tip out the contents gently and carefully separate the new plants. Put them into 3–4 inches (7.5–10cm) pots of potting compost and grow them on at least until the roots have filled the pot before planting them out in the garden.

Root cuttings

Small pieces of the roots of some perennials have the ability to produce complete new plants. This can be a nuisance – when you are trying to replace an old clump with something else, for example. But you can also make use of it to increase your stock.

Lift the plants in late autumn or early spring and remove a few of the strongest roots. Those that are of the thick, fleshy type (such as dicentra) should be cut into sections about 3 inches (7.5cm) long. Insert them vertically into pots containing a mixture of peat, sand and soil, and cover them with ½ inch (12mm) of sand (Figure 11). Thinner roots are cut into similar sections but laid horizontally.

When shoots about 2 inches (5cm) long have formed, pot the new plants up individually and grow them on until they are ready to plant out.

Rose cuttings

Most modern bush roses are 'budded' on to vigorous rootstocks from wild roses, because they themselves would not make a good root system. You cannot, therefore, get similar new plants from cuttings. However, cuttings from many shrub and climbing roses which are grown on their own roots will

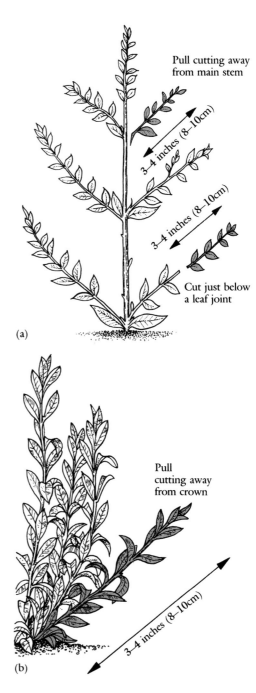

Pull cutting away from main stem

3–4 inches (8–10cm)

3–4 inches (8–10cm)

Cut just below a leaf joint

(a)

Pull cutting away from crown

3–4 inches (8–10cm)

(b)

Figure 9. Taking soft-stem cuttings.

Remove leaves from bottom half of cutting

6 inch (15cm) pot

1:1 mixture of peat and sand plus 1 teaspoon calcified seaweed

Figure 10. Rooting soft-stem cuttings.

produce vigorous plants.

In early September, cut lengths about 10 inches (25cm) long from shoots that have grown during the previous summer (Figure 12). Remove all the leaves except the top two or three and insert the cuttings 9 inches (23cm) apart into a narrow trench in a sheltered, partly shaded, place. Firm them in well and leave them until the next autumn when those that have rooted can be planted out.

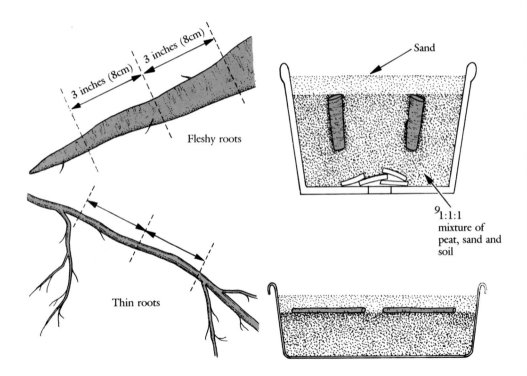

3 inches (8cm)

3 inches (8cm)

3 inches (8cm)

Fleshy roots

Thin roots

Sand

9 1:1:1 mixture of peat, sand and soil

Figure 11. Taking root cuttings.

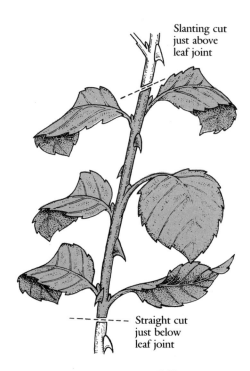

Slanting cut
just above
leaf joint

Straight cut
just below
leaf joint

Figure 12. Taking rose cuttings.

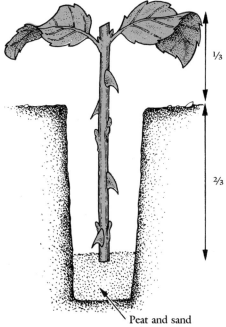

¹/₃

²/₃

Peat and sand

CHAPTER 4
ANNUALS AND BIENNIALS

Annuals are plants which grow from seed, flower and then die all in one season. *Biennials* also die when they have flowered, but their life is spread over two seasons: only leaves grow in the first year; flowers appear in the second.

Annuals and biennials, therefore, must be continually cleared away and replaced – creating work but also giving many advantages. They can provide quick colour to the new garden or fill temporary gaps in borders and beds. They provide variety – you can afford to experiment with something different each year if you want to, and the seed catalogues offer a surprisingly large range to choose from.

Annuals are usually described as being either 'hardy' or 'half-hardy'. *Hardy annuals* are those that can be sown directly outside in spring, and you must grow them yourself from seed (see Chapter 3). Examples are nasturtiums (*Tropaeolum*), sunflowers (*Helianthus*), and sweet peas (*Lathyrus*). *Half-hardy* annuals are the familiar 'summer bedding' plants such as lobelia and petunias. They need a warmer start if they are to make a worthwhile display before the autumn, and to raise them successfully yourself you need a greenhouse. Alternatively, you can buy them for planting out when all danger of frost has passed.

Biennials are the plants that give an early spring display. They are usually sown in early summer, either in the greenhouse or in a seed bed outside, and transplanted to their flowering positions in September and October. Mullein (*Verbascum*) and honesty (*Lunaria*) are true biennials; the most familiar spring bedding plants – wallflowers (*Cheiranthus*), pansies (*Viola*) and sweet williams (*Dianthus*) are in fact perennials but are treated as biennials for convenience because their quality deteriorates in subsequent years.

You will also find blurred distinctions between the other categories of plants. Some summer bedding plants, such as antirrhinums, are perennials. The hardiest annuals, like cornflowers (*Centaurea*), can be sown in autumn to provide earlier blooms the next year, and catalogues sometimes disagree on whether an annual should be classed as hardy or half-hardy: some French marigold (*Tagetes*) varieties, usually used as bedding plants, can be sown *outdoors* in May and still flower well. Treat the descriptions as merely telling you how the plants should be grown rather than botanical definitions and you should not get confused.

Using annuals and biennials
Annuals and biennials provide interest for a relatively short time, so large areas of them are inappropriate for small gardens. The bedding schemes of half-hardy annuals seen in public parks are showy, but expensive and time-

consuming. Hardy annuals can similarly be used to fill whole beds; they are cheap (the only cost is the packets of seed), but it is not easy to plan an attractive, lasting display.

Annuals and biennials are, however, ideal for filling gaps: in spaces left by spring bulbs in a flower bed, between young shrubs and immature herbaceous plants, or as an edging to a mixed border. They take little from the soil and as long as you avoid tall swamping varieties, they will not present harmful competition to other plants. Seed catalogues offer annuals and biennials of every conceivable size: tall or short, bushy or sprawling, climbing or trailing – for every place and purpose. Those, such as honesty, that are too large and untidy for a formal garden can often be left to self-seed in wilder areas.

If you like flowers on your vegetable patch, hardy annuals are the best to choose, as they can be sown and cleared with the crops. 'Intersowing' flowers amongst the crop plants is not easy to plan, if the one is not to interfere with the other. However, it is simple to sow along the edges of beds or in unused patches. The effect is pleasing to look at and can benefit the crop (see page 116). Half-hardy annuals are ideal for window boxes, tubs and hanging baskets.

Whether you are planting up a whole bed or just filling in gaps, annuals and biennials look best in bold groups rather than dotted round the garden. In general you need tall plants in the middle of an island bed or at the back of a border, but do not make the bed look too regimented. The traditional bedding schemes use edging plants like alyssum or lobelia, behind which come gradually taller ones – perhaps petunias or African marigolds (*Tagetes*). However, you can produce equally striking arrangements by using one type of plant in varieties of different colours and/or size. With hardy annuals, the problem comes in predicting how large they will grow. The heights given on the seed packets can be particularly misleading: they seem to vary a lot with soil conditions and climate. You really need to know the height and habit of each variety in your own garden to make an

Table 4: Annuals and biennials which need or tolerate special growing conditions.

Prefer neutral or alkaline soil	Prefer acid soil	Tolerate poor soil	Need moist well-composted soil	Tolerate light or partial shade
Callistephus	Clarkia	Alyssum	Asperula	Asperula
Cheiranthus	Nemesia	Calendula	Begonia	Begonia
Chrysanthemum		Echium	Digitalis	Bellis
Dianthus		Eschscholzia	Impatiens	Calendula
Gypsophila		Linaria	Lathyrus	Campanula
Lathyrus		Malcomia	Lobelia	Impatiens
Matthiola		Tropaeolum	Mimulus	Lobelia
Reseda			Myosotis	Lunaria
Scabious			Nemophila	Malcomia
			Zinnia	Mimulus
				Moluccella
				Myosotis
				Nemophila
				Nigella
				Viola

Table 5: Seasons in which some common annuals and biennials start to flower.

Early spring	Mid spring	Late spring	Early summer	Midsummer
Anchusa	Cheiranthus	Alyssum	Centaurea	MOST
Bellis	Myosotis	Campanula	Dianthus barbatus	OTHER
Calendula	Lunaria	Iberis	Digitalis	ANNUALS
Viola	Malcomia	Limnanthesa	Echium	AND
		Matthiola incana	Hesperis	BIENNIALS
		Papaver nudicaule	Verbascum	

Some flowers which last until the first frosts:

Ageratum, Ameranthus, Antirrhinum, Calendula, Callistephus, Clarkia, Echium, Impatiens, Malope, Nicotiana, Rudbeckia, Petunia, Salvia, Scabious, Tagetes, Tropaeolum

accurate plan for a large hardy annual bed. Those with a bushy habit which do not need staking are the best for mixed borders.

Growing conditions

Most annuals will grow well in any ordinary well-drained garden soil: they do not need fertilizers or compost, and, in fact, a rich soil may give too many leaves and too few flowers. Most also prefer a sunny spot, but there are some you can find for moist and/or shady places. Some do better on limy soils and some on acid soils. Examples are given in Table 4.

All season colour

Annuals and biennials alone cannot provide colour throughout the year. Spring sown annuals contribute little until June, and by early October are beginning to look tatty. Nevertheless, many biennials can provide welcome blooms in early spring: wallflowers and forget-me-nots (*Myosotis*) are the most familiar examples. Try choosing less common varieties from the seed catalogues rather than buying plants: dwarf varieties, for example, make a striking display with spring bulbs.

The other way to get early blooms is to sow the hardiest annuals in autumn, or make use of self-sown seedlings: this only applies in mild areas as losses are likely to be high in severe winters. At the other end of the summer, some annuals such as petunias and marigolds will bloom until the first hard frosts: regular dead-heading will help keep them going. The occasional pansy may be seen in flower right through mild winters. Examples of early and late flowering annuals and biennials are given in Table 5.

Scent

Nearly all the annuals and biennials that are scented have become popular flowers, the favourite deservedly being sweet peas.

Sunshine brings out the rich scent of wallflowers, the musky smell of mignonette (*Reseda*), and the honey-like scent of alyssum. However, in the evening the air in the garden becomes more heavily perfumed: the flowers of night-scented stocks (*Matthiola*), evening primroses (*Oenothera*) and traditional varieties of tobacco plant (*Nicotiana*) open up, and the spicy scent of sweet williams becomes more noticeable.

Less well-known scented plants are *Asperula azurea*, an annual relative of the native woodland woodruff, and the

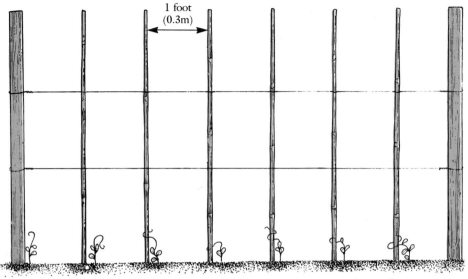

1 foot
(0.3m)

Secure the canes to
wires stretched between
two posts – one cane
for each plant

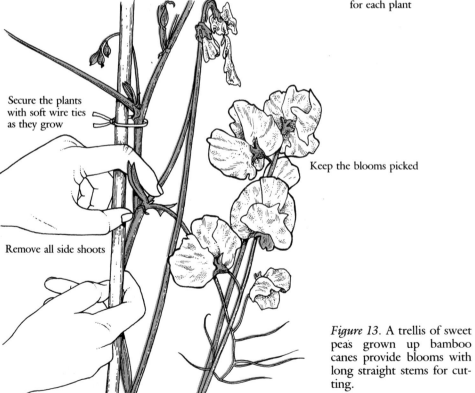

Secure the plants
with soft wire ties
as they grow

Keep the blooms picked

Remove all side shoots

Figure 13. A trellis of sweet peas grown up bamboo canes provide blooms with long straight stems for cutting.

old-fashioned bedding plant cherry-pie (*Heliotrope*).

Check the catalogue descriptions carefully when you are buying seeds of scented annuals as not all modern varieties – bred for other desirable characteristics such as bigger flowers and a wide range of colour – retain the scent of the originals. For example, the sweet pea varieties described as 'old-fashioned' are reliably highly fragrant, as is the white tobacco plant *Nicotiana affinis*.

Cutting

Many of the summer annuals make good cut flowers. Those described above that open only at night and those that open only in sunshine (such as the sun plant *Portulaca*) should be avoided, but most others are worth a try. Even the short-lived poppies (*Papaver*) can be used if they are picked while in bud and the cut ends seared in a flame. Amongst the most outstanding are the annual asters, for lasting displays, and gypsophila (sometimes aptly called 'baby's breath') whose frothy white flowers provide an excellent foil for any large colourful blooms.

Those annuals and biennials that can be used in dried arrangements are also good value: the 'everlasting' straw flowers (*Helichrysum*), shell flowers (*Moluccella*) and sea lavender (*Statice*). Honesty also comes into this category for its array of flat silvery seed pods, as similarly do love-in-a-mist (*Nigella*), teasels (*Dipsacus*) and poppies.

For decoration of a different kind, you might grow the *edible* annuals: the flowers of borage (*Borago*), nasturtiums, pot marigolds and the tiny heartsease pansies (*Viola*); these can be used variously in salads, sweet dishes and drinks.

Annuals grown specially for cutting fit well in the vegetable garden: here they can be well cared for and staked unceremoniously to ensure good blooms on straight stems. Sweet peas on a netting trellis or – for the enthusiast – on individual canes (Figure 13) make an attractive temporary screen.

Wildlife

Many of the old cottage garden plants that bees and butterflies love are hardy annuals or biennials – most still available in seed catalogues. They are colourful and simple, whereas in new 'double' flowered varieties the pollen and nectar are concealed by close clusters of petals.

Colour advertises what the flower has to offer. Long-tongued bees favour blue and purple blooms which often have nectaries deep in the flower: borage, echium, nigella, cornflowers and canterbury bells (*Campanula*), for example. Insects with shorter tongues, such as hoverflies, need flat open flowers where the nectar and pollen are easily accessible – often white or yellow daisy-like flowers: pot marigolds, poached-egg plant (*Limnanthes*) or the annual rudbeckia. The open blue and white nemophila and annual convolvulus are also amongst their favourites. Many pale fragrant flowers such as evening primroses and tobacco plants which open towards dusk attract night-flying moths.

The early flowering biennials, such as wallflowers, forget-me-nots and honesty, are particularly valuable, for they provide the first nectar for newly emerging insects. Honesty is also a food plant for the caterpillars of the orange-tip butterfly. At the other end of the season, the seed heads of sunflowers and teasels provide food for the birds.

Native plants are always worth growing alongside 'exotic' species – both for their own sake and for the added support they may give to insect life. A few such annuals and biennials are still available in seed catalogues as garden flowers, although these are usually cultivated varieties. Examples are given in Table 6.

Buying seeds and plants

Seeds

Wherever you buy your seeds, it is a good idea to study one or two seed catalogues to see the range of varieties (some offer over 500 annuals and biennials). Often less than a third of these will be on sale in shops, and for something unusual it is worth ordering directly from the seedsman. Just because varieties are not on general sale it does not mean they are difficult to grow or inappropriate to the ordinary garden.

The catalogue should give you useful information that you need in order to plan. You should try to find out the sowing time and temperature; the colour, height and flowering time; the position and soil conditions the plant prefers, and whether there is anything special about the variety. Bear in mind, however, that varieties described as 'new' are often only slightly different to established ones, and although 'award winning' varieties will undoubtedly be good, others may be equally so – and more suited to *your* garden. F_1 hybrids are varieties produced from two parent varieties that have been inbred to make them uniform. This uniformity is of great value to parks departments, for example, for producing large bedding displays. However, it is less important to gardeners at home, particularly since F_1 seed is expensive. It should germinate readily and give vigorous plants, but so usually does ordinary seed. 'Pelleted' seed is coated with an inert material which makes it easy to handle. It is also expensive: the idea is to sow it accurately so there is little wasted. It can, however, be difficult to germinate – you *must* keep the soil moist until the seedlings emerge. Only a very limited number of annuals and biennials are available in this form.

Table 6: Native annuals and biennials as garden flowers.

Agrostemma githago	Corncockle	'Milas' is the common garden variety.
Centaurea cyanus	Annual cornflower	Many varieties – avoid double flowers.
Digitalis purpurea	Foxglove	Some of the garden varieties look fairly close to the species.
Echium vulgare	Viper's bugloss	The native species can be obtained but common garden varieties are most likely to be of *E. plantagineum*.
Iberis amara	Wild candytuft	The more commonly sold similar species is *I. umbellata*.
Myosotis sylvatica *Myosotis alpestris*	Forget-me-not	Many good garden varieties.
Papaver rhoeas	Corn poppy	Garden varieties derived from this are 'Shirley poppies'.
Viola tricolor	Heartsease	Native species available.

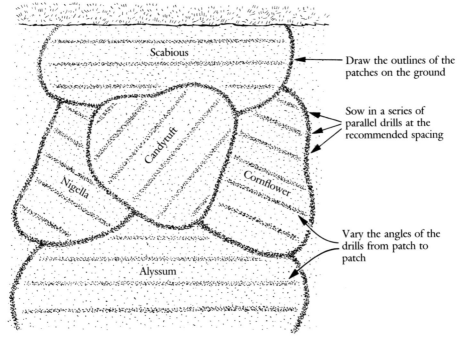

Figure 14. Sowing annual flowers. Single straight lines are acceptable for edging plants or cut flowers in the vegetable garden, but elsewhere irregular patches look more natural.

Seedlings

Some of the big seed firms now post out seedlings of a few bedding plant varieties. These are useful if you find it difficult to provide the right conditions for seeds to germinate (many do best at temperatures around 20°C). However, you must have enough light and frost-free space to grow on the seedlings in pots or trays – they are not ready to transplant outside.

Plants

Most shops and garden centres have a range of 'bedding plants' (half-hardy annuals) on sale in spring and autumn – usually in trays divided up into strips, although wallflowers, stocks and sweet williams may be bare-rooted. Choice is limited compared to the hundreds of varieties available from seed, and the plants will work out much more expen-

sive. Labelling is often poor too: it may be difficult to predict their colour and height, and you could end up with something completely unsuitable.

Nevertheless, buying bedding plants is one of the quickest and easiest ways to add colour to the garden. Be critical in your choice: avoid buying plants that look drawn or starved, or that are limp through lack of moisture. If you can, buy them early and look after them well yourself until it is time to plant them out.

Sowing, planting and growing

When to sow

Annual flowers are usually sown in spring, directly into the patches where they are to grow. You can broadcast the seed and rake it in, but this makes weeding difficult – especially if you are

Use individual canes for the stems of large flowers, securing them with soft twine tied tightly around the cane and loosely around the plant.

Use twiggy sticks for flimsy plants. Put them in when the plants are small, bending them inwards, so that they are covered by subsequent growth.

Figure 15. Giving support to annual flowers.

not certain what the young flower seedlings look like! It is usually better to sow them in a series of short drills within each patch (Figure 14). Some of the hardiest can be sown in autumn to give early blooms the following year.

Biennials are usually sown in late summer in pots or in a seed bed outside. Half-hardy annuals must be sown in the warm in early spring. (The sowing methods are described in detail in Chapter 3.)

When to plant

Whether you have raised them yourself or bought them, half-hardy annuals must not be planted out until late May or early June – after the last frost in your area. They should be 'hardened off' for up to a week beforehand by leaving them outside during the day and bringing them back in at night. Biennials are usually planted in their final positions in September or October.

Spacing

Spacing can vary from 6 inches (15cm) for edging plants such as lobelia to 2 feet (0.6m) for tall bushy wallflowers. Guidelines are given for selected plants at the end of the chapter, but there are no strict rules. Small bedding plants placed close together give an impressive show more quickly without any ill effects, but tall ones suffer if they are overcrowded.

Planting out

Choose a dull, still day for planting, or wait for the cool of the evening. Soak the plants well beforehand – this is as important as watering them afterwards. For each plant, make a hole large enough to take the roots without cramping them, then tap the plant gently from its pot or lift it from a tray with a trowel. Holding the root ball at soil level, fill in the earth around the roots, firming it well. Water the plants immediately and then every day or two in dry weather until they are established.

After care
All the plants will need careful hand-weeding and hoeing until they grow large enough to cover the soil. A few tall, top heavy plants may need staking: use twiggy pea sticks for bushy plants, (put in *early* so that the plants can grow up and hide them), and bamboo canes for single flower spikes (see Figure 15.) Where it is practical, remove the flower heads as they fade: the plant's energy will then go into making more and better blooms rather than producing seed.

Pests and diseases
Annuals and biennials that you raise yourself from seed should be healthy plants and with proper care have every chance of remaining that way. However, a few common pests and diseases can be a problem. This section deals with the most likely offenders and the varieties most at risk. Details of symptoms and control measures are given in Chapter 2.

Slugs can be devastating, particularly to young bedding plants such as petunias and marigolds in wet conditions. For a few plants, covering them with individual lemonade-bottle 'cloches' as described in Figure 4 is a reliable answer; otherwise try less susceptible plants such as lobelia, or very hardy annuals such as *Limnanthes* sown in drier autumn conditions. A well-drained sunny site, as preferred by most annuals, should be the *least* popular with slugs!

The other ubiquitous pest – aphids – should not be too much of a problem with healthy plants. Greenfly may affect seedlings and sweet pea blooms early in the season. The problem of blackfly on

nasturtiums can be hopeless – but fickle (affecting some plants and not others, in some years and not others).

Pea and bean weevil – a common pest in the vegetable garden – can also affect sweet peas, making notches in the leaves. This should not harm healthy mature plants but seedlings may be badly damaged. Plants like stocks, wallflowers and alyssum that belong to the Cruciferae family share some pests and diseases with cabbages and sprouts. Flea beetle may attack the seedlings and mature plants can be infected by clubroot if this disease is present in the soil.

Any annuals and biennials can be affected by the common fungal diseases like botrytis and mildews, but they usually only become a problem in adverse conditions. Useful avoidance measures are described in Chapter 2. You may find some petunias particularly prone to botrytis (grey mould), and antirrhinums, sweet peas, poppies and wallflowers are more likely to suffer from downy mildew; forget-me-nots are commonly seen with powdery mildew. Rust is a more specific disease, particularly affecting antirrhinums, hollyhocks and sweet williams. This is one reason why these plants – which are perennials in the right conditions – are grown as biennials.

A selection of annuals and biennials
Details are given here of the annuals and biennials used in the plans in Chapter 8. These are just examples, chosen because they have at least one of the qualities mentioned in Chapter 1 (lasting interest, scent, resistance to disease, attraction to wildlife, etc.).

ALYSSUM
(*Alyssum maritimum*, Cruciferae)
A hardy annual. Low growing 3–6 inches (7.5–15cm) and spreading to 8–12 inches (20–30 cm). Flowers are

commonly white, but rose and purple varieties are available. They have a faint but noticeable sweet honey scent. Excellent for edging beds and for pots and rockeries.

Flowering period—May–September.

Growing conditions—Any ordinary well-drained soil, full sun.

Propagation—Sow seeds indoors in pots in March or outdoors where they are to flower in April. Often self-seeds.

Pests—Flea beetle may attack young seedlings outdoors.

BABY BLUE EYES
(*Nemophila insignis,* Hydrophyllaceae)
A hardy annual. Low and spreading, height and spacing 6 inches (15cm). Flowers are sky blue with a white centre. A useful edging or carpeting plant for shady conditions, much liked by bees and hoverflies.

Flowering period—June–September.

Growing conditions—Moist soil, partial shade.

Propagation—Sow seeds in flowering position in March, or in September in mild areas.

BABY'S BREATH
(*Gypsophila elegans,* Caryophyllaceae)
A hardy annual, height 18 inches (45cm), spacing 1 foot (30cm). A delicate branching plant with frothy sprays of tiny flowers in white or pink. Invaluable for flower arrangements.

Flowering period—June–September.

Growing conditions—Any well-drained garden soil, preferably alkaline; sunny position.

Propagation—Sow seeds in flowering position in March, or in September in mild areas.

CANTERBURY BELL
(*Campanula medium,* Campanulaceae)
A biennial. Most varieties are about 2–3 feet (0.6–1.0m) high, but there are dwarf ones 1½ feet (45cm); spacing 1 foot (30cm). Large bell-shaped flowers are carried on long stems, in shades of blue, pink and violet, and white. The variety 'Cup and saucer' is semi-double, the outer petals making a distinct 'saucer'. Campanula is an old cottage garden plant, much loved by bees

Flowering period—May–July.

Growing conditions—Well drained, fairly fertile soil; sunny or mostly sunny spot. Tall varieties need staking.

Propagation—Sow seeds outdoors in a nursery bed or pots in late spring.

EVENING PRIMROSE
(*Oenothera biennis,* Onagraceae)
A biennial. Height 2–3 feet (60–90cm), spacing 1 foot (30cm). Large pale yellow flowers on long stems open in the evening; strongly scented. Suitable for the back of a border or a wild garden; attracts night-flying moths.

Flowering period—June–October.

Growing conditions—Well-drained soil (the plants will tolerate fairly dry conditions); sunny position.

Propagation—Sow seed outside in a nursery bed or pots, July–August.

Pests—Can be affected by eelworm.

FORGET-ME-NOT
(*Myosotis* sp, Boraginaceae)
Varieties of *M. sylvatica* and *M. alpestris* are usually grown as biennials, although they can last two or three years. They are bushy plants normally growing to 1 foot (30 cm) although dwarf varieties grow only up to about 8 inches (20cm). The native types have small light blue flowers, but cultivated varieties can have deep blue, white, or deep pink flowers. Useful for wild gardens and for bedding.

Flowering period—March–June.

Growing conditions—A moist soil containing plenty of organic matter is best, although forget-me-nots will grow in most ordinary soils; partial shade.

Propagation—Sow seeds outdoors in a nursery bed or in pots, May–July. Readily self-seeds.

Diseases—Suffers from powdery mildew if under stress, particularly in dry conditions.

FOXGLOVE

(*Digitalis purpurea*, Scrophulariaceae)
Generally biennial, but can be perennial under ideal conditions. The wild types grow to 3–4 feet (1.0–1.3m) and have spires of purple, pink or white flowers which hang down one side of the stem. 'Excelsior' hybrids are the ones often listed; they have a wider colour range and carry the flowers horizontally around stems up to 5 feet (1.6m) long. 'Foxy' is a useful dwarf strain, growing to 2½ feet (75cm), with flowers in fairly natural colours. Space plants 1½–2 feet (45–60cm) apart. A useful border or wild garden plant, good for cutting.

Flowering period—June–August.

Growing conditions—Moist soil containing plenty of organic matter; partial shade.

Propagation—Sow seed in midsummer outside in a nursery bed or pots. Seeds of 'Foxy' can be sown indoors in March to give flowers in the first year. Wild types readily self-seed.

HOLLYHOCK

(*Althaea rosea*, Malvaceae)
A short-lived perennial, best grown as a biennial, although some dwarf varieties can be grown as annuals. Spires of wide funnel-shaped blooms grow from 2–8 feet (0.6–2.4m) tall, spacing 15–24 inches (38–60cm), in shades of yellow, red, pink and white. Most varieties are mixtures of colours; many have double flowers but single ones are available. A classic cottage garden plant; useful for the back of borders

Flowering period— July–September.

Growing conditions—Prefer a rich soil and sheltered sunny spot. Tall varieties may need staking.

Propagation—To grow as a biennial, sow seeds outside in a nursery bed or pots in June–July. To grow as an annual, sow in pots in heat (13°C) in February.

Pests—Caterpillars of various moths eat the leaves, but not usually to a devastating proportion.

Diseases—Rust can be a problem, but is worse on plants left as perennials.

HONESTY

(*Lunaria biennis*, Cruciferae)
A biennial. Bushy plants, height 2–2½ feet (60–75cm), spacing 1 foot (30cm). Flowers are commonly purple, but sometimes white; there are also forms with variegated leaves. The variety 'Munstead purple' is fragrant. Honesty is an old cottage garden plant, useful for early flowers at the back of a border or in a wild garden. The flat seed pods are attractive when dry.

Flowering period—April–June.

Growing conditions—Any well-drained garden soil; does well in partial shade.

Propagation—Sow seeds outdoors in a nursery bed or pots, May or June.

Diseases—Do not plant on land affected by clubroot.

LOVE-IN-A-MIST

(*Nigella damascena*, Ranunculaceae)
A hardy annual. Height about 18 inches (45cm), spacing 9 inches (23cm). Finely cut 'misty' foliage surrounds blue, white or purple flowers (the common variety is blue). Loved by bees; both flowers and seed pods used in flower arrangements.

Flowering period—July–September.

Growing conditions—Any well-drained garden soil; sunny position.

Propagation—Sow in flowering position in March, or in September in mild areas. Often self-seeds.

MIGNONETTE
(*Reseda odorata*, Resedaceae)
A hardy annual. Upright and bushy, height 12–15 inches (30–38cm), spacing 9 inches (23cm). The species has small creamy flowers in clustered heads, strongly fragrant; a few garden varieties have larger flowers tinged with red. A classic cottage garden plant, good for bees and for cutting.

Flowering period—July–September.

Growing conditions—Any reasonable alkaline garden soil will do, but enrich with compost for best results. Sunny position.

Propagation—Sow seeds in April where they are to flower, or in pots indoors in March for transplanting.

NASTURTIUM
(*Tropaeolum majus*, Tropaeolaceae)
A hardy annual. Trailing or climbing varieties spread over 6 feet (2m). Semi-trailing or 'gleam' varities form bushy plants to a height of about 15 inches (38cm) and later throw out runners; useful for hanging baskets. Dwarf or 'Tom thumb' varieties form compact plants, height about 9 inches (23cm), spread about 1 foot (30cm). Flowers come in a range of reds, oranges and yellows; a few varieties are double and 'Alaska' has cream variegated leaves. The leaves smell and taste peppery, and the flowers smell faintly the same; both make an attractive and tasty addition to salads.

Flowering period—June–September.

Growing conditions—Most flowers are produced on poor soil in a sunny position

Propagation—Sow seeds outdoors in April or in pots indoors in March for transplanting. Will often self-seed.

Pests—Blackfly are a common problem.

PANSY
(*Viola* × *wittrockiana*, Violaceae)
Short-lived perennials, usually grown as annuals or biennials. Height 6–9 inches (15–23 cm); spacing 9–12 inches (23–30cm). Garden pansies are bred from the tiny-flowered native heartsease *Viola tricolor*, but many have flowers up to 4 inches (10cm) across. Their colour range is wide and often a mixture of colours make up the typical pansy 'face' (violas are a different species, similar in appearance, but usually single-coloured and more compact). Pansies are useful for bedding, pots, gaps in borders, and underplanting roses.

Flowering period—Autumn intermittently until the main flowering period – this depends on variety.

Growing conditions—Moist soil containing plenty of organic matter is ideal. Sun or partial shade.

Propagation—Sow in a nursery bed or pots outside in June or July for autumn planting, or in March indoors for earlier flowering.

Diseases—Fungal rots sometimes attack the bases of the stems (described as 'pansy sickness').

PETUNIA
(*Petunia* × *hybrida*, Solanaceae)
The numerous garden varieties are grown as half-hardy annuals. They are spreading plants, height and spacing 6–12 inches (15–30cm) with large trumpet flowers in shades of white, cream, pink, red, mauve and blue; a few are two-coloured and some double. 'Grandiflora' types have very large flowers; 'multiflora' types have large numbers of smaller flowers that are more weather resistant. F_1 hybrids are more vigorous and are usually available as single colours which are better for

small bedding schemes. Their trailing nature makes them good for tubs and hanging baskets. The flowers of single varieties are much loved by bees.

Flowering period—June–October.

Growing conditions—Ordinary well-drained soil; sunny sheltered position.

Propagation—Sow in heat in March; seed is tiny and young plants very tender.

Pests—Slugs are very fond of young plants.

Diseases—Foot rot can be a problem.

POACHED EGG FLOWER

(*Limnanthes douglasii*, Limnanthaceae)
A hardy annual. Bushy plants with pale green ferny leaves, height 6 inches (15cm), spacing 4 inches (10cm). Flowers are yellow with white edges – as the name suggests. A useful edging plant, favourite with bees and hoverflies.

Flowering period—May–June for autumn-sown plants; June–August for spring-sown plants.

Growing conditions—Any ordinary garden soil; sunny position.

Propagation—Sow seeds in flowering position in March or September. Readily self-seeds.

POT MARIGOLD

(*Calendula officinalis*, Compositae)
A hardy annual. The traditional varieties grow up to 2 feet (60cm) and have large flat single flowers in bright oranges and yellows. Most new varieties have double flowers and many are compact – only about 1 foot (30cm) tall. A cheerful border plant, good for cutting, the petals are edible and can be used to decorate salads.

Flowering period—May until the first frosts.

Growing conditions—Grows in poor soil; sun or partial shade.

Propagation—Sow seeds in Septem-

ber or March where they are to flower. Self-seeds readily.

Pests—Slugs and cutworms are fond of the seedlings.

Diseases—Powdery mildew can be a problem in dry conditions.

SUNFLOWER

(*Helianthus annus*, Compositae)
A hardy annual. Varieties range from the giants – single heads on 9 foot (3m) stems to dwarf 3 foot (1m) branching plants. Golden yellow is the typical sunflower colour, but they can come in shades from pale primrose to bronzy red.

Flowering period—July–September.

Growing conditions—Any well-drained garden soil will do although compost will help the giants reach their maximum size; sunny position. Tall varieties need staking.

Propagation—Sow seeds where they are to grow in late April, or a few weeks earlier in pots for planting out in May.

Pests—Slugs are fond of the young plants.

SWEET PEA

(*Lathyrus odoratus*, Leguminosae)
A hardy annual. Tall varieties climb to about 7 feet (2.1m), low-growing varieties to about 2–3 feet (60–90cm); spacing 6–12 inches (15–30cm). Flowers are in both bold and pastel shades of crimson, blue, pink, mauve and white. The 'old-fashioned' small-flowered varieties are very sweetly scented; most tall varieties listed are named 'Spencer' varieties with larger flowers and a very wide range of colours – good for cutting, but not all are as fragrant. Low growing varieties are best in beds and borders.

Flowering period—June–September.

Growing conditions—A good, well-drained, slightly alkaline soil gives best results: incorporate well-rotted manure or compost in the autumn before planting. Open, sunny position. Tall varieties need support from canes or netting; pea sticks are sufficient for low varieties. Water in dry weather and dead-head regularly to encourage blooms.

Propagation—Sow seeds in pots in a cold greenhouse (16°C) in October or March. Soak varieties with hard black seeds overnight and/or nick the seed coat to help germination. Pinch out the tips of seedlings when they are 4 inches (10cm) high to encourage strong side growths. Plant out in April or May. Seeds can also be sown outside in April, but mice are fond of them!

Pests—Slugs and pea weevils attack seedlings. Aphids and thrips can affect mature plants.

Diseases—Yellowing plants may be affected by fusarium wilt or foot rot. Virus diseases can cause a variety of symptoms, and sweet peas are also very susceptible to the effects of chemical weedkillers (persisting in straw, for example) which cause distortion and stunting.

SWEET WILLIAM
(*Dianthus barbatus,* Caryophyllaceae)
Short-lived perennials, best grown as biennials. Short varieties 6–12 inches (15–30cm) are good for bedding; taller ones up to 2 feet (60cm) for borders and cutting; spacing 8–10 inches (20–25cm). They have heads of small flowers in shades from dark red to pink, often with white markings; richly scented. Most varieties are mixtures.

Flowering period—June–July.

Growing conditions—Any ordinary well-drained soil that is not too acid; sunny position.

Propagation—Sow seeds May–June outside in nursery beds or pots.

Diseases—Can be affected by leaf spot (grey or brown spots) and rust.

TOBACCO PLANT
(*Nicotiana* sp, Solanaceae)
N. affinis is the traditional type, grown as a half-hardy annual although it can overwinter in favourable positions. Height 3 feet (90 cm), spacing 1 foot (30cm). The species has white tubular flowers, strongly fragrant, opening in the evening, and there are garden varieties with flowers of cream, pink, crimson and yellow. Some newer dwarf hybrids, height 9–12 inches (23–30cm), have flowers which remain open all day, but they are not necessarily so scented.

Flowering period—June–September.

Growing conditions—Well-drained and composted soil; warm sheltered position in sun or light shade.

Propagation—Sow seeds in February or March in pots in heat (18°C).

Pests—Aphids and slugs attack young plants.

CHAPTER 5
BULBOUS PLANTS

The term 'bulb' is often used to include 'corms', 'tubers' and 'rhizomes' as well as true bulbs, and will be used in this way here unless a distinction is necessary. These are all storage organs of plants and are treated in similar ways in the garden, although they are botanically distinct as shown in Figure 16. Together they can provide reliable all-year-round interest to the garden with relatively little work.

Bulbs contain all that is necessary to give new plants a good start and are an ideal way of obtaining them: many can be lifted and stored quite safely for short periods. You then merely need to plant them at the right depth and at the right time and wait. There is little to go wrong! However, during the growing period they must replenish their exhausted food supply for the coming year – so their future performance does depend on caring for them properly.

Besides the familiar spring bulbs, there are many other bulbous plants which are equally easy to grow and well worth making extra effort to obtain

Using bulbous plants

Many bulbous plants are hardy and can be readily 'naturalized' – that is, they can be left in the ground year after year to grow and multiply. They do best when grown like this. Suitable places where they will be undisturbed include: grassy areas, the ground under de-

ciduous trees and shrubs, along hedge bottoms, and uncultivated parts of borders or rock gardens.

Bulbous plants that are not reliably hardy must be lifted and stored, otherwise you will lose some – if not all – of your stock. Familiar examples are garden tulips, dahlias and gladioli, but there are many more. So if you are not prepared for the extra work this entails, read catalogue descriptions carefully before you buy.

Bulbs naturalized in grass

You must allow at least six weeks between the time that the flowers of your bulbs fade and mowing the grass. Thus for lawns where mowing begins in April only the earliest flowering bulbs are suitable: winter aconites (*Eranthis*) and snowdrops (*Galanthus*). Dutch crocuses (which are the best type of crocus for growing in grass) come slightly later. For an area left unmown until early summer your choice can include spring snowflakes (*Leucojum*), Star-of-Bethlehem (*Ornithogalum*) and many types of daffodil. Snakeshead fritillaries (*Fritillaria meleagris*) also naturalize well in grass, but do not flower until early May. At the other end of the year, mowing only until August allows you to grow the autumn-flowering meadow saffron (*Colchicum* – sometimes misleadingly called 'autumn crocus') and true autumn crocuses such as *C. speciosus*.

Bulbs naturalized under deciduous trees and large shrubs

Note how early your trees and shrubs come into leaf, since spring bulbs must flower and fade before the canopy becomes too dense. Aconites and snow-drops are suitable here also, and you can add the early blue flowers of *Chionodoxa* and *Scilla*, which are not generally vigorous enough to succeed in grass. A woodland area or shrubbery where the soil is good will suit anemones (those such as the native wood anemone *A. nemorosa*), dog's tooth violet (*Erythronium*) and, of course, bluebells. Dutch crocuses and daffodils will do reasonably well provided it is not too shady, although they do best in full sun. A few species of lily will also grow in a semi-shaded wild area amongst trees, provided that it is well drained. However, this means that the grass or undergrowth must be left untrimmed from mid-spring until autumn. *Lilium martagon* is a suitable, easily obtainable, variety. Many other lilies will grow in the partial shade of a shrub border.

For autumn and winter, no plant gives as much value as the hardy cyclamen (*C. hederifolium* and *C. coum*). Once established, they will do well around the bole of a large tree or at the base of a hedge – any place where the soil is bare and it is dry and shady. Their flowers appear in early autumn and the attractively patterned leaves last through the winter, never looking tatty.

Bulbs in the rock garden

A rock garden shows small delicate spring bulbs to their best advantage. Varieties of crocuses such as *C. chrysanthus* and *C. sieberi* are better here than in grass – some are very early flowering. Snowdrops, chionodoxa, scillas, spring snowflakes and dwarf irises such as *I. reticulata* are all suitable. Later blooms can include dwarf tulips and narcissi.

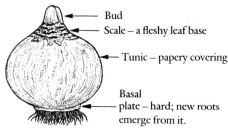

Bud
Scale – a fleshy leaf base
Tunic – papery covering
Basal plate – hard; new roots emerge from it.

True bulb: e.g., daffodil, lily.

Corm: swollen stem base with papery covering and basal plate out of which roots grow; e.g., crocus, gladioli.

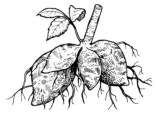

Tuber: a swollen underground stem or root; e.g., anemone, foxtail lily (*Eremurus*), begonias and dahlias.

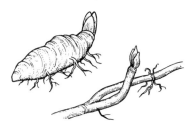

Rhizome: thickened stem, growing horizontally along or just below the soil surface; e.g., lily-of-the-valley.

Figure 16. Bulbs, corms, tubers and rhizomes.

Bulbs in mixed borders

It is not so easy to naturalize bulbs in borders where plants are lifted regularly, and the ground cultivated and manured. However, they can be put in odd undisturbed corners or amongst small shrubs and long-standing perennials. Spring-flowering bulbs are most effective where neighbouring plants will grow to hide their dying foliage. Summer-flowering bulbs will fill the time between the spring flowers of shrubs and their autumn colour: lilies, in particular, appreciate some shade and protection at their base even if their tops are in the sun, and so are well suited to growing up amongst low-growing shrubs or perennials. Autumn-flowering bulbs, such as nerines, provide end-of-season interest as summer perennials are cut back.

Spring-flowering bulbs also mix well with bedding plants, as these are shallow rooted and take little from the soil. Well-tried schemes (but still worth copying!) include red or yellow tulips with forget-me-nots, and mixed pansies with daffodils.

Grouping of bulbs

Whether you are planting bulbs in borders, under trees or in grass, set those of one kind together in large enough numbers to make a bold impression – the smaller the blossoms, the more you will need. Mixing two or more kinds in a single group looks unnatural. In the wild, you would see a clump where the bulbs had multiplied with perhaps a few dotted around nearby which had grown from seed.

Growing conditions

The essential condition for nearly all bulbous plants is good drainage: very few will tolerate damp places, although many need a soil that contains plenty of organic matter so that it remains moist without waterlogging. Their food requirements are less than many garden plants, so you should use peat or leaf mould to improve a heavy soil and well-rotted compost on a light soil – never fresh manure.

In the wild, the storage organs of bulbous plants are often very necessary for their survival – enabling them to 'sit out' a period of extreme drought, heat, cold or darkness. This means they can often be used in problem areas of the garden where conditions are too harsh for other plants. Sunshine and moisture *are* necessary – but only during their natural growing period. Thus spring bulbs flourish under deciduous trees and nerines will flower in autumn at the base of a dry wall.

Summer-flowering bulbs are the most fussy: many are not at all winter hardy or need a warm sheltered spot in order to survive. Even the hardy ones included in this chapter benefit from watering and mulching during dry spells – this particularly applies to lilies. There are also many tall varieties among the summer bulbs – *Lilium henryi*, for example, grows up to 8 feet (2.5m) – and these must be protected from strong winds.

The growing conditions of a variety of bulbs are outlined in Table 7.

All-year-round colour

From these many ways of using bulbous plants, you can see that they will give you flowers almost all year round. The approximate flowering times are given in Table 8. Spring bulbs are the most valuable – providing colour, despite snow and ice, when few other plants dare to bloom. But almost as welcome are the burst of fresh blooms in autumn provided by nerines, hardy cyclamen and autumn crocuses, which can survive well beyond the first frost. A few of the tender summer bulbs are worth the extra work for their spectacular blooms and long flowering periods, but for the less ambitious, or simply busier gardener, there are those such as alliums and hardy lilies that need virtually no attention.

You can often extend the flowering period of any particular type of bulb by using a combination of varieties: for example, by planting some of the 'cyclamineus' group of narcissi and some of the 'poeticus' group, as well as ordinary daffodils, you can have narcissi in bloom over six weeks or more. In addition, those planted in full sun will usually bloom earlier than those in partial shade

Irises of one kind or another can be found in flower during most months of the year. The 'reticulata' irises – dwarf plants growing from bulbs – bloom in very early spring, while *I. stylosa* can be found in flower throughout a mild winter. (This iris belongs to the 'beardless' iris group which have slender underground rhizomes rather than bulbs, and are often classified as herbaceous plants.)

Scent

Bulbous plants provide some of the favourite rich perfumes: hyacinths and lily-of-the valley (*Convallaria*), for example. Lilies have the same reputation, although not all are scented and some, in fact, have a disagreeable smell! The Madonna lily (*L. candidum*), for example, has a particularly heavy scent – almost too overpowering for some – and *L. regale* and *L. henryi* are popular strongly scented species. The smell of *L. martagon*, however, is not so pleasant. The summer hyacinth (*Galtonia*) is scented (although not as strongly as the commonly seen spring hyacinths), and so is the tiny hardy cyclamen (*C. purpurascens*) which flowers in early autumn.

The scent of the small spring bulbs is less noticeable, but distinctly present for those willing to kneel in the garden at this time of year! The catalogues list certain varieties as particularly fragrant, such as the winter aconite (*Eranthis tubergenii*), the snowdrop (*Galanthus nivalis* 'S. Arnott'), and the 'reticulata' irises (*I. danfordiae* and *I. reticulata*).

Table 7: Bulbous plants that will grow well under particular conditions.

Acidity	Dry and sunny position	Moist well-drained soil	Light shade from deciduous trees or shrubs
Cammassia	*Allium* sp	*Anemone* sp	*Colchicum* sp
	Crocosmia sp	*Convallaria majalis*	*Convallaria majalis*
Soil not too acid	*Iris* (bearded)	*Fritillaria meleagris*	*Cyclamen* sp
Iris (bearded)	*Iris* (reticulata)	*Galanthus* sp	*Eranthis* sp
Iris (reticulata)	*Muscari* sp	*Leucojum* sp	*Endymion* sp
Lilium (some species; e.g., *L. candidum*)	*Nerine bowdenii*	*Lilium* sp, e.g., Bellingham hybrids	*Erythronium* sp
Tulipa sp	*Tulipa* sp		*Galanthus* sp
			Galtonia candicans
			Leucojum sp
Acid soil		**Permanently moist soil**	*Lilium* (e.g., *L. henryi*, *L. martagon*, *L. regale*)
Lilium (some species, e.g. Bellingham hybrids)		*Camassia*	*Narcissi* sp
			Ornithogalum sp
			Scilla sp

Table 8: Seasons when common hardy bulbs start to flower.

Winter	Early spring	Spring	Late spring
Cyclamen coum	*Anemone* sp ♦	Convallaria majalis ♦	Iris sp (e.g., *germanica*
Crocus sp ♦	*Chionodoxa* sp	*Endymion* sp ♦	and hybrids)♦
Eranthis hyemalis ♦	*Crocus* (Dutch)♦	*Fritillaria meleagris*	Narcissus sp (e.g.,
Galanthus sp ♦	*Eranthis tubergenii*	*Leucojum aestivum* ♦	'Poeticus')
Iris (reticulata)	*Erythronium* sp ♦	*Muscari* sp ♦	*Tulipa* sp (e.g.,*greigii*) ♦
	Galanthus sp	*Narcissi* (many) ♦	
	Leucojum vernum ♦	*Ornithogalum* sp ♦	
	Tulipa sp ♦	*Tulipa* sp ♦	
	(e.g., *kauffmannia*)	(e.g., *fosteriana*)	
	Narcissus sp ♦		
	(e.g. *cyclamineus*)		
Early summer	**Midsummer**	**Late summer**	**Early autumn**
Allium sp (many) ♦	*Allium* sp (e.g.,	*Cyclamen purpurascens* ♦	*Colchicum* sp ♦
Camassia sp ♦	*sphaerocephalum*)	*Galtonia candicans* ♦	*Crocus speciousus* ♦
Iris sp (e.g.,*pallida*	*Crocosmia* sp ♦	*Lilium* sp (e.g., *henryi*) ♦	*Cyclamen hederifolium* ♦
and hybrids)	*Lilium* sp (e.g.,		*Nerine bowdenii*
	martagon)		

♦ = the plant flowers from this time onwards

Following these come the narcissi: the jonquils and some of the 'poeticus' group of narcissi, such as 'Old Pheasant's Eye'.

Cutting
The flowers of bulbs, with their long straight stiff stems, often make fine flower arrangements. Spring flowers are particularly welcome indoors, but soon fade because of the contrast in temperatures. These bulbs lend themselves well to growing in pots and this is a much better alternative for a lasting display. In summer, irises and lilies are frequently grown for big displays.

Wildlife
All the spring bulbs provide valuable nectar and pollen for emerging insects. However, as for annuals and biennials, choose single rather than double varieties, as the food is more accessible in these; similarly, the small-cupped narcissi may be useful to a wider range of insects than the long-trumpeted daffodils.

A number of bulbs commonly grown in gardens are, in fact, native species or closely related varieties, and therefore particularly merit a place. Examples are given in Table 9.

Buying bulbous plants
It is possible to grow some bulbous plants from seed, but they could take as long as four or five years to flower and they may not 'come true' – that is, they may not resemble the parent plant. There are exceptions: some lilies and cyclamen will flower within a year; alliums and crocuses sometimes in two years. And the variability of the plants can be part of the excitement of doing-it-yourself. However, in general it is better to start by buying bulbs since they are relatively cheap and also relatively foolproof! They can quickly increase in numbers if they are naturalized, and you can often propagate from them yourself (see Chapter 3).

Garden shops generally have a good selection of spring-flowering bulbs; however, before making a purchase, check to see that they are accurately labelled so that you know exactly what

Table 9: Native bulbs as garden flowers.

Anenome nemorosa	–	wood anemone
Colchicum autumnale	–	meadow saffron
Convallaria majalis	–	lily-of-the-valley
Endymion nonscriptus	–	bluebell
Fritillaria meleagris	–	snakes-head fritillary
Galanthus nivalis	–	snowdrop (may be naturalized)
Leucojum aestivum	–	summer snowflake
Leucojum vernum	–	spring snowflake (may be naturalized)
Narcissus pseudonarcissus	–	wild daffodil
Ornithogalum umbellatum	–	star-of-Bethlehem (may be naturalized)

you are getting. Crocuses, for example, should be labelled 'Dutch' or given the species name and, preferably, the name of the variety too. Mail-order suppliers will almost certainly be more expensive, but will have special varieties and some of the less common summer-flowering and autumn-flowering bulbs such as camassias and nerines. Sometimes you can buy quantities of daffodils or crocuses 'for naturalizing' which are cheaper, but a percentage of them may be small and will not necessarily flower in their first year. 'Mixtures' containing different varieties – different colours of crocus or types of daffodil, for example – may also be cheaper; however, they neither look so natural nor have such impact, especially in a small garden.

When buying bulbs over the counter, select those which are firm, healthy and of a good size (Figure 17). They should *not* have started into growth. Since the conditions in shops are often less than ideal, it is a good idea to buy your bulbs as soon as they come in and store them in the cool until the weather is right to plant them. Lilies do not store well and should be planted straightaway. If this is not possible, pot them up individually

Figure 17. Choosing bulbs.

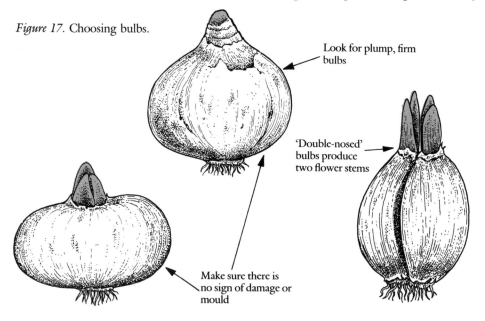

Look for plump, firm bulbs

'Double-nosed' bulbs produce two flower stems

Make sure there is no sign of damage or mould

and store them in a cool dry place until spring.

Planting

When to plant

Spring-flowering bulbs are nearly all sold in the autumn for planting before Christmas, the main exception being snowdrops which are best planted in spring, just after they have flowered (these are thus sometimes difficult to buy in good condition). Summer-flowering bulbs are planted in either autumn or spring, depending on when the plant does most of its growing. Autumn-flowering bulbs are usually planted in spring or summer. (Check with the selection of bulbous plants at the end of the chapter for details.)

Spacing and depth

Bulbs usually look their best when flowering in groups – and the smaller the plants are, the closer together within the group they should be: say about 3 inches (7–8cm) for aconites and up to 8 inches (20cm) for daffodils. For a natural effect (with daffodils in a lawn, for example), plant a few individual bulbs irregularly round each main group and they, will look as if they have seeded them-selves.

The correct depth to plant bulbs depends both on the variety and the soil. A rough guide for most true bulbs and corms is given in Figure 18. However, there are exceptions to this, and there is no general rule at all for tubers and rhizomes, so check details

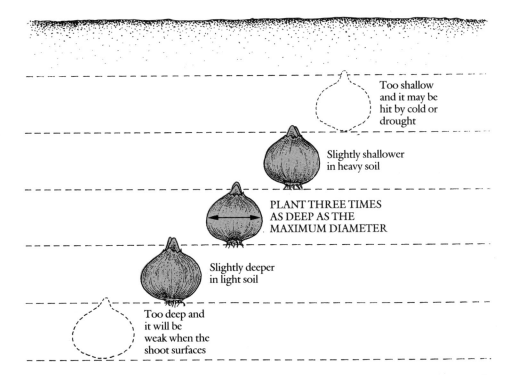

Too shallow and it may be hit by cold or drought

Slightly shallower in heavy soil

PLANT THREE TIMES AS DEEP AS THE MAXIMUM DIAMETER

Slightly deeper in light soil

Too deep and it will be weak when the shoot surfaces

Figure 18. Depth for planting true bulbs and corms.

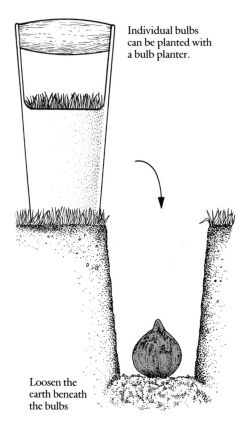

Individual bulbs can be planted with a bulb planter.

Loosen the earth beneath the bulbs

For groups of bulbs, dig a hole with a spade.

Figure 19. Bulb planting methods.

with the last section in this chapter before planting. With lilies, the planting depth depends on whether they are 'stem-rooting' (that is, whether they produce roots from their stems as well as from their bulbs) – these types must have about 5 inches (12cm) of soil above the bulbs, otherwise they could starve.

Planting methods

In borders where the soil is loose, individual bulbs can be planted with a trowel. In turf a bulb-planter that removes a plug of soil can be useful, but loosen the soil in the bottom of the hole with a trowel as well, and make sure there are no air pockets (Figure 19).

For groups of bulbs, use a spade to dig a square hole which gives enough room to space the individual bulbs out. Loosen the soil below the planting depth; mix in sand, peat or leafmould if it is very heavy and about two table-spoons of bonemeal if it is very poor.

Care of naturalized bulbs

Naturalized bulbs usually put on a brave show however much they are neglected, but, nevertheless, they will repay a little extra care.

First, the leaves *must* remain on the plant for as long as possible after it has flowered: this is when they are making the food that provides next year's blooms. Wait until they have turned completely brown if possible, and never tie them in a knot as this prevents the nutrients going back into the bulb. You can usually mow grass containing naturalized bulbs about six weeks after their flowers have faded.

In borders, keep the plants well weeded, as it is important not to let perennial weeds become established. This usually means hand weeding while the plants are growing and *light* hoeing after they have died down. It is a good idea to mark the areas containing bulbs from one year to the next: use plastic labels or small pieces of bamboo cane. You thus avoid disturbing them during winter and spring plantings, and run less risk of hoeing off the emerging shoots in spring

Staking will only be necessary for very tall flowers, like galtonia and some lilies. The spikes are often secured individually to wire stakes or bamboo canes as for annuals (see Figure 15). Remove flowerheads as soon as they fade where this is practical.

The soil may need replenishing from time to time, especially where there is competition from trees and shrubs. This is best done by mulching with leaf-mould or well-rotted compost in autumn, with a scattering of bonemeal on poor soils. Avoid fresh manure or fertilizers containing nitrogen as these just encourage lush foliage. A covering of straw in winter will protect the less hardy bulbs in cold places. If, after a few years, the bulbs have multiplied and become so crowded that they produce smaller or fewer blooms, you should lift them and replant the largest. Small 'offsets' can be used to increase your stock (see Chapter 3).

Pests and diseases

There are pests and diseases that will attack bulbs both in the ground and in store. Some are familiar garden pests but there are several that you will find only on bulbous plants. Details of symptoms and control are given in Chapter 2. Luckily, few are troublesome in most gardens, especially where the bulbs are naturalized.

It is particularly important to examine bought bulbs carefully for signs of attack by bacteria and fungi. Fungal growth on daffodils could be 'smoulder' and on tulips 'tulip fire'. Soft fungal rots can affect any bulb, corm or tuber, and dry rots sometimes affect corms. Iden-

tification may be difficult, but since no diseased bulb will produce a healthy plant, you should throw away any that are suspect.

Specific bulb pests include the narcissus fly (which can attack snowdrops, irises and some other bulbs as well as narcissi) and bulb eelworms (whose targets include narcissi, hyacinths, snowdrops and tulips). Symptoms can be seen on leaves and bulbs (see Table 1.) Other soil pests such as vine weevil, chafer grubs and wireworms will also attack all bulbs, but damage is not usually significant in bulbs that are naturalized. Swift moth caterpillars may damage the rhizomes of irises and lily-of-the-valley.

Few pests attack the foliage or flowers of bulbous plants. However, as always, slugs are fond of the young shoots – lilies suffer to a greater extent than most. Greenfly are occasionally a problem in late spring and early summer, more because they carry virus diseases than from the damage they do. Lilies and summer tulips are particularly susceptible to such diseases (which can cause stunting and distortion of the leaves and flowers) but no plant is immune. A few nurseries guarantee that their lily stock is 'virus-free'. Other streaks and distortion of summer flowers can be caused by thrips. (See Tables 1 and 2 on pages 23–30 for descriptions of pests and diseases and recommended methods of control.)

A selection of bulbous plants

BLUEBELL
(*Endymion* sp, Liliaceae)
The familiar native bluebell is *E. nonscriptus*, height about 9 inches (23cm); the Spanish bluebell *E. hispanicus* is similar but has broader leaves and flowers. There are white and pink varieties of both species. They natural-

ize well not only under trees but in open areas – grass or borders.

Flowering period—April–June.

Growing conditions—Moist, but well-drained soil containing plenty of organic matter. Sun or light shade. Plant August/September – as soon as available because the bulbs easily shrivel and go mouldy in store. Depth 4–6 inches (10–15cm), spacing 4 inches (10cm).

Propagation—Lift and divide established clumps of bulbs when flowers have died down; some offsets are produced. They will also spread by self-sown seedlings, but these are slow to flower.

Diseases—Rust can occasionally be a problem.

CROCUS
(*Crocus* sp, Iridaceae)

Many species of crocus flower in spring and a few in autumn. The popular Dutch or 'large flowered' crocuses (*C. vernus* hybrids) flower in March; they have golden yellow, purple, white or striped blooms, height 3–5 inches (7.5–12.5cm), and are suitable for naturalizing in borders or short grass. Other species, such as the many named varieties of *C. chrysanthus* (purple, white and yellow flowers), *C. sieberi* and *C. tomasinianus* (mauve flowers) start flowering in February; they rarely reach more than 3 inches (7.5cm) high and look best in rockeries or tubs and pots. The autumn flowering *C. speciosus* has named varieties in shades of blue and white, height 4–5 inches (10–12.5cm); it naturalizes readily in borders and short grass

Flowering period—See above.

Growing conditions—Almost any well-drained soil; will grow in light shade, but the flowers will open more in a sunny sheltered spot. Planting time for most species is September–October, earlier for autumn flowering species.

Depth about 3 inches (7.5cm), spacing 3–4 inches (7.5–10cm).

Propagation—Divide overcrowded clumps in autumn; separate cormlets. Slow to flower from seed and hybrids do not come true.

Pests—Corms may be particularly prone to damage from soil pests and mice. Birds peck the flowers.

Diseases—Dry rot may affect the corms.

DAFFODIL, NARCISSI
(*Narcissus* sp, Amaryllidaceae)

The many narcissi species and garden varieties have a familiar flower, characterized by a central trumpet surrounded by six petals. For horticultural purposes, narcissi are divided into eleven groups and they will sometimes be listed in this way in catalogues.

Daffodils are in the first group: defined as varieties having a trumpet as long as or longer than the outer petals; height 1–1½ feet (30–45cm). Those such as 'Golden Harvest' are the traditional yellow colour, but all-white varieties such as 'Beersheba' are very attractive; these varieties are good for naturalizing in rough grass, beneath shrubs or in borders.

Other narcissi are grouped according to the length of the trumpet, whether the flowers are double or single and the number of flowers per stem. Many are two-coloured: for example, orange trumpets and white petals. They are best chosen on individual merit. Worth looking out for are 'jonquils' which have dark tubular leaves and strongly scented flowers – best planted in warm sheltered places. The 'poeticus' narcissi are late flowering – generally more useful in borders rather than grass; the variety 'Pheasant's Eye' is scented. 'Cyclamineus' narcissi have distinctive long cups, petals swept back, and narrow leaves – often early flowering.

Many of the groups contain dwarf varieties suitable for rockeries and tubs; some are only 3 inches (7.5cm) tall, but most are around 6 or 7 inches (17cm). The native daffodil *N. pseudonarcissus* is pale yellow, about 9 inches (23cm) high, flowers April.

Flowering period—March–May depending on variety.

Growing conditions—Thrive in fairly rich, well-drained soil; sun or light shade. Plant in August–September at a depth three times the depth of the bulb; spacing 4–8 inches (10–20cm) for tall varieties; 2–3 inches (5–7.5cm) for dwarf varieties.

Propagation—Lift and divide congested clumps in early autumn; separate offsets. Garden varieties do not come true from seed.

Pests—Eelworm and narcissus fly larvae can attack the bulbs.

Diseases—Narcissus fire can affect the foliage, and there are also several narcissus virus diseases.

FLAG IRIS
(*Iris germanica*, Iridaceae)
I. germanica and its hybrids form one of the groups of irises which grow from thick rhizomes on the surface of the soil. (Other groups have thin creeping or fibrous rhizomes, and yet others like *Iris reticulata* grow from bulbs.) They have fans of stiff light green sword-shaped evergreen leaves. The flower of *I. germanica* is blue/purple with lighter markings, sweetly scented, height 2 feet (60cm); the hybrids have a great range of height and colour. Their contrasting foliage and early summer flowers make them a useful border plant.

Flowering period—May.

Growing conditions—Fairly good, well-drained soil that is not too acid: an open sunny position. Plant late June–early September, 1 foot (30cm) apart, with the rhizome top just showing.

Propagation—Divide rhizomes after flowering or in September.

Pests—Swift moth caterpillars may damage the rhizomes.

Diseases—Can be affected by leaf spot and rhizome rot in poor conditions.

GLORY OF THE SNOW
(*Chionodoxa* sp, Liliaceae)
The common species is *C. luciliae* which has light blue starry flowers with white centres, but there are also white and pink forms; height 6 inches (15cm). *C. gigantea*, violet blue, is slightly larger; *C. sardensis*, bright blue, is slightly smaller and later flowering. All naturalize well in rock gardens, at the front of borders or in short grass.

Flowering period—February/April.

Growing conditions—Any ordinary well-drained soil, sunny position. Plant in autumn, 2–3 inches (5–7.5cm) deep, about 3 inches (7.5cm) apart.

Propagation—Divide clumps when leaves die down in May and replant immediately. Can be grown from seed sown as soon as it is ripe.

GRAPE HYACINTH
(*Muscari* sp, Liliaceae)
The familiar species are *M. armeniacum* and *M. botryoides*, height about 8 inches (20cm). They have grassy leaves and tiny deep blue globular flowers densely clustered at the top of the flower stems. There are also named varieties, with flowers in different shades of blue and white. They are useful at the front of borders and for edging beds, but can be invasive.

Flowering period—April–May.

Growing conditions—Any well-drained soil; flowers best in full sun. Plant September–November at a depth of about 3 inches (7.5cm), spacing 3–4 inches (7.5–10cm).

Propagation—Divide clumps in autumn or sow seeds in late summer after they have ripened.

HARDY CYCLAMEN
(Cyclamen sp, Primulaceae)*
There are several hardy species of cyclamen – miniature versions of the familiar pot-plant; height 3–4 inches (7.5–10cm); the leaves often have atractive silvery markings and remain long after the blooms have faded. *C. purpurascens* has strongly scented carmine flowers, July–September. *C. hederifolium* has mauve, pink or white flowers, August–November, leaves are nearly always patterned; *C. coum* has carmine, pink, or occasionally white flowers, December–March, leaves are sometimes plain. These species are invaluable for their winter flowers and all-year-round attractive foliage, especially in bare areas under trees or shrubs.

Flowering period—See above.

Growing conditions—Well-drained soil containing plenty of organic matter. Shady, sheltered position. Plant August–September 1–2 inches (2.5–5cm) deep, 6 inches (15cm) apart. Mulch with peat after flowering.

Propagation—The corms do not produce offsets, but may self-seed. Alternatively, collect seeds when they ripen and sow pots in a cool greenhouse or cold frame. They should flower in their second year.

LILY
(Lilium sp, Liliaceae)*
Some of the many lilies available deserve their reputation for being difficult to grow, but there *are* those which are easy and reliable. The most familiar example is the species *L. regale*, which has white trumpet-shaped flowers with a yellow throat, strongly fragrant, height 3–5 feet (1–1.5m), and is useful for herbaceous and shrub borders. Those in the hybrid strain 'African Queen' have similar orange flowers, strongly fragrant, height 4–5 feet (1.2–

1.5m). 'Corsage' is equally reliable, with open cream flowers spotted red; fragrant, height 3–4 feet (1–1.2m), popular for flower arrangements. The species *L. martagon* has purple/pink 'turk's cap' flowers, height 3–4 feet (1–1.2m); its scent is not very pleasant but, nevertheless, it is useful for naturalizing in a wild area.

Flowering period—*L. martagon* June–July; *L. regale* and 'Corsage' July; 'African Queen' July–August.

Growing conditions—A well-drained soil is essential, enriched with leafmould, peat or well-rotted compost. All the types listed here do well in semi-shade; *L. regale* and 'Corsage' can also be planted in full sun but often grow better if their bases are shaded by low-growing plants. Plant early autumn if possible. Do not let bulbs dry out. *L. martagon* is basal rooting, so plant shallowly, about 2 inches (5cm) deep. The other types are stem rooting, so plant about 6 inches (15cm) deep. Mulch in spring and water during dry periods in summer. Tall types need staking in exposed positions.

Propagation—Divide congested clumps between October and March. *L. regale* can be grown easily from seed.

Pests—Aphids are the worst pests – spoiling the flowers and also transmitting virus diseases. Lily beetle may be a problem in the south. Slugs attack young shoots.

Diseases—Lilies are prone to virus diseases and to botrytis, although the types described here are among the least susceptible.

LILY OF THE VALLEY
(Convallaria majalis, Liliaceae)*
The common species has pairs of wide leaves and arching stems carrying a number of small white bell-shaped flowers; height 6–8 inches (15–20cm). There are named varieties with double

7. Single flowers – in this case of a peony – are much more accessible to insects seeking nectar and pollen.

8. The useful autumn-flowering 'ice-plant' *(Sedum spectabile)* is particularly attractive to butterflies.

9. The development during the growing season of a border containing mainly herbaceous planting:

(a) In early spring – very bare except for a few bulbs and primulas.

(b) Early summer – the border has filled out with astrantia (the pink flowers in the foreground), herbaceous geraniums and irises in flower; the variegated and purple sages at the front of the border have become bushy.

(c) Midsummer – no bare patches to be seen; the astrantia is still in flower together with the goatsbeard *(Aruncus,* the white plumes in the background) and the roses.

(d) Late summer – colour now comes from mauve phlox and orange crocosmia. The white spires of the late-flowering summer hyacinth (*Galtonia*) are just visible.

10. This border contains no shrubs – only herbaceous plants. Edging plants include lady's mantle (*Alchemilla*) and catmint (*Nepeta*); height is obtained with delphiniums and cardoons.

11. The perennial pea (*Lathyrus latifolius*) climbs into other wall plants and gives good midsummer colour.

(a)

(b)

(c)

13

12. (a) A formal paved rose garden with small beds of individual varieties, each edged with other plants to give interest and diversity to the garden.
(b) A bed of the yellow 'Arthur Bell' edged with mauve campanula.
(c) 'Alec's Red' with garden pinks.

13. The large single rose 'Complicata' climbs around the garden gate.

and pink flowers. All are sweetly scented. Excellent for putting under trees in wild areas or in cool shady corners.

Flowering period—April–May.

Growing conditions—Soil containing plenty of organic matter; partial shade. Plant rhizomes in September or October, 1 inch (2.5cm) deep, 3–4 inches (7.5–10cm) apart. They spread quickly in good conditions.

Propagation—Lift and divide rhizomes from October to March.

Diseases—Grey mould can affect foliage in wet conditions.

MEADOW SAFFRON/AUTUMN CROCUS
(*Colchicum* sp, Liliaceae)

Commonly available autumn-flowering species are *C. autumnale* (the native species) and *C. speciosum*. Both have crocus-like' flowers, height about 6 inches (15cm), which are stemless – the petals form a long thin tube into the soil. The flowers of the species are mauve, but there are white and rose varieties. The leaves appear after flowering and can be untidy in borders, but colchicums are useful for autumn colour in rough grass.

Flowering period—September–November.

Growing conditions—Well-drained soil containing plenty of organic matter; sun or light shade. Plant July–September 4 inches (10cm) deep, 9 inches (23cm) apart. If planted in rough grass, stop mowing in August and do not restart before June.

Propagation—Divide established clumps of corms in June and July, and separate cormlets. Very slow to germinate and flower from seed.

MONTBRETIA
(*Crocosmia* sp, Iridaceae)

The hybrids *C.* × *crocosmiiflora* are the true montbretias, height about 2 feet (60cm), spacing 4–6 inches (10–15cm); the corms give clumps of sword-shaped leaves and bright tubular flowers on wiry stems; colour yellow/orange/red depending on variety. *C. masonorum*, height about 2½ feet (75cm), has larger orange flowers on arching stems. They are all useful late-flowering plants in a border; good for flower arranging; *C.* × *crocosmiiflora* will also hold its own in a wild area.

Flowering period—July – September.

Growing conditions—A light well-drained soil and a sunny sheltered spot are essential if the plants are to thrive. Plant in March about 3 inches (7.5cm) deep. Leave the dead leaves on the plant until March to give the corms winter protection.

Propagation—Divide clumps in autumn after flowering or in early spring.

NERINE
(*Nerine bowdenii*, Amaryllidaceae)

This is the only hardy species of nerine. It has clusters of large pink flowers, borne on leafless stalks: the strap-shaped leaves appear soon afterwards. Height 1–2 feet (30–60cm), planting distance 6 inches (15cm). Useful for late colour in a mixed border.

Flowering period—September–October.

Growing conditions—Any well-drained soil, sunny position – best in a sunny border against a wall. Plant August or April, 4 inches (10cm) deep.

Propagation—Lift, divide and replant overcrowded clumps in late spring.

ORNAMENTAL ONIONS
(*Allium* sp, Liliaceae)

Many species are hardy, easy-to-grow summer flowering bulbs. The flower umbels are often globular – like bolted leeks or onions but brightly coloured –

on stiff stems. Heights range from the giant 4 foot (1.3m) to the dwarf 9 inches (23cm). The flowers are mostly pink, blue or purple although *A. moly* is yellow. Useful for borders are *A. albophilosum*, 18–24 inches (45–60cm), with large striking umbels of starry lilac flowers and *A. moly*, 12 inches (30cm), with small heads of yellow flowers. For the rockery, *A. ostrowskianum*, about 9 inches (23cm), has dainty pink flowers. All three bloom in June. Most alliums are long lasting when cut fresh and can be dried for winter arrangements.

Flowering period—May–July, depending on species.

Growing conditions—Any reasonable well-drained soil, best in full sun. Plant September–October at a depth three times the height of the bulb. Spacing 4–12 inches (10–30cm), depending on height of plant. Tall species may need staking.

Propagation—Divide established clumps in spring or autumn and replant immediately. Bulbils can be separated. Many species can be grown quite quickly from seed, sown in pots as soon as it ripens in early autumn, or in spring.

Diseases—Can be affected by white rot.

QUAMASH
(*Camassia* sp, Liliaceae)
These are amongst the easiest summer flowering bulbs to grow. Their flowers are blue, white or purple; small starry blooms clothe the top of tall flower spikes. *C. esculenta* is the original 'quamash' with edible bulbs, height about 2½ feet (75cm). *C. leichtinii* is often recommended as the best to grow, height 3 feet (90cm). They are useful for naturalizing in damp areas: in borders, amongst shrubs or in damp grass in wild areas.

Flowering period—June–July.

Growing conditions—Best in heavy moist soil, sun or partial shade. Plant September/October, about 4 inches (10cm) deep, 4–6 inches (10–15cm) apart.

Propagation—Divide established clumps in autumn and replant immediately; separate offsets. Slow to flower from seed.

'RETICULATA' IRISES
(*Iris reticulata* and *Iris danfordiae*, Iridaceae)
The 'Reticulata' irises are amongst the few types of iris that grow from bulbs rather than rhizomes. They have tubular deep green leaves. *Iris danfordiae*, height 4 inches (10cm) has yellow scented flowers, and is the earliest to bloom. *Iris reticulata*, height 6 inches (15cm), has blue/purple scented flowers with yellow markings.

Flowering period—February–March.

Growing conditions—Light well-drained limy soil; sunny position. Plant in September–October, 2–3 inches (5–7.5cm) deep, 4 inches (10cm) apart.

Propagation—Lift and divide clumps when foliage has died down; separate offsets.

Pests—Bulbs can be affected by eelworm and narcissus fly larvae.

SNAKE'S HEAD FRITILLARY
(*Fritillaria meleagris*, Liliaceae)
A rare native plant of waterside meadows; height about 1 foot (30cm). Delicate leaves, and large bell-shaped flowers hanging singly or in pairs from the top of each stem. These commonly have a distinctive white and purple chequered pattern, although some are pure white and there are named garden varieties in different shades of purple. They can be grown in rockeries, at the front of borders or naturalized in grass as long as this is not mown until July.

Flowering period—April–early May.

Growing conditions—A reasonably fertile moist, but well-drained, soil; fairly sunny position. Plant September–November, 4–6 inches (10–15cm) deep, about 5 inches (12.5cm) apart. Do not let the bulbs dry out and surround them with coarse sand in the planting hole to help drainage if necessary.

Propagation—Will self-seed, or seeds can be collected and sown in pots as soon as they are ripe. Some bulblets may be produced, in which case you can propagate from these.

SNOWDROP
(*Galanthus* sp, Amaryllidaceae)
G. nivalis is the common native or naturalized snowdrop, height about 5 inches (13cm). The flowers are white with green markings on the three short inner petals. There are named varieties with different markings; 'Flora-plena' has double flowers; 'S. Arnott' is scented and more vigorous, growing up to 10 inches (25cm) high. *G. elwesii* may also grow to this height. Both species are good for naturalizing in grass under trees.

Flowering period—January–March.

Growing conditions—Best in fairly rich moist soils in light shade. Plant in spring just after flowering if possible, rather than using dry bulbs in autumn; planting depths 4 inches (10cm), spacing 3–6 inches (7.5–12cm).

Propagation—Divide established clumps just after flowering and replant immediately. The species also spread by seed, but plants are slow to mature.

Pests—Bulbs can be affected by eelworms and by narcissus fly larvae.

Diseases—Botrytis can affect the leaves in bad conditions.

SNOWFLAKE
(*Leucojum* sp, Amaryllidaceae)
Snowflakes resemble tall snowdrops, but their flowers are more rounded – all six petals are the same size. The spring snowflake *L. vernum*, height 8 inches (20cm), spacing 3–4 inches (7.5–10cm), flowers in February and March. The summer snowflake *L. aestivum*, height 2 feet (60cm), spacing 6–8 inches (15–20cm) flowers in April and May. Snowflakes are probably native plants and naturalize easily in borders; spring snowflakes will also grow in short grass with other spring bulbs.

Flowering period—See above.

Growing conditions—Best in moist soil; sun or light shade. Plant August–September, 3–4 inches (7.5–10cm) deep. Leave undisturbed for several years.

Propagation—Divide overcrowded clumps as the leaves die down; replant immediately. Offsets and viable seeds are produced, but plants are very slow to mature.

SQUILL
(*Scilla* sp, Liliaceae)
Spring-flowering squills are dwarf plants with starry blue flowers: *S. bifolia* – height about 5 inches (10cm), deep blue flowers lightening to pale blue in the centre; *S. sibirica* – height about 4 inches (10cm), brighter blue flowers which are less open; *S. tubergeniana* – similar, but pale blue. All are good for naturalizing in short grass, under trees or on rockeries.

Flowering period—March.

Growing conditions—Moist, but well-drained, soil; sun or light shade. Plant early autumn, 2–3 inches (5–7.5cm) deep, about 3 inches (7.5cm) apart.

Propagation—Divide clumps as the leaves die down. Can be very slow to flower from seed.

Pests—Bulbs can be affected by eelworm.

Diseases—Leaves can be affected by rust.

STAR OF BETHLEHEM
(*Ornithogalum* sp, Liliaceae)
Two species are native or long-naturalized in Britain: *O. nutans* has nodding bell-shaped flowers and *O. umbellatum* flat starry flowers. Both are white, marked with pale green, on stems 8–12 inches (20–30cm) tall. They grow easily – under trees, in summer-mown grass and in borders, although *O. umbellatum* can be invasive. *O. balansae* is only about 5 inches (12cm) high, good for rockeries.

Flowering period—O. balansae March–April; others April–May.

Growing conditions—Any ordinary well-drained soil. *O. balansae* must have sun, but the other two species also thrive in partial shade. Plant October, 2 inches (5cm) deep, planting distance 4–6 inches (10–15cm).

Propagation—Divide clumps in summer when leaves die down; replant at once. Bulblets can be separated. Sow seeds in pots when they ripen, or in early autumn.

SUMMER HYACINTH
(*Galtonia candicans*, Liliaceae)
Galtonia is like a tall elongated hyacinth: white bell-shaped flowers are carried up stems 3–4 feet (1–1.2m) high, but they are only slightly fragrant. Suitable for the back of a herbaceous border or between early flowering shrubs.

Flowering period—August–September.

Growing conditions—Ordinary soil, sun or light shade. Plant March–April, 6 inches (15cm) deep, 12 inches (30cm) apart. Dislikes disturbance.

Propagation—Not easy; a few offsets may be produced.

TULIP
(*Tulipa* sp, Liliaceae)
Nearly all tulips have the characteristic goblet-shaped flowers carried singly on stiff stems. The best for naturalizing are varieties of the three smaller species. *T. kaufmanniana*, height 5–10 inches (12–25cm) depending on variety, is very early flowering, with blooms mostly two-coloured in shades of yellow, red, pink and cream; leaves may be patterned with purple. *T. fosteriana*, height 10–15 inches (25–38cm), flowers in April; mainly scarlet although there are some yellows. *T. greigii*, height 5–15 inches (12–38cm), flowers in April; mainly red. All these tulips are good for flowering with spring bedding or for providing early colour in a mixed border. They will flower for many years, slowly increasing in numbers, whereas other tulips will gradually deteriorate even in good conditions.

Flowering period—See above.

Growing conditions—A well-drained soil is essential, preferably one that is alkaline; best in a sunny, sheltered spot. Plant in November, 6 inches (15cm) deep, 6–9 inches (15–23cm) apart.

Propagation—From offsets; slow from seed and garden varieties do not come true.

Pests—Bulbs and stems of young plants are often damaged by slugs. Eelworms may affect stems and bulbs.

Diseases—Tulips are susceptible to 'tulip fire' (a grey bulb rot), and also to several virus diseases.

WINDFLOWER/WOOD ANEMONE
(*Anemone* sp, Ranunculaceae)
A. nemerosa is the native wood anemone, height 6–8 inches (15–20cm), which has white single daisy-like flowers; there is also a blue form. It is good for naturalizing in open woodland. *A. blanda* is similar, slightly smaller and earlier flowering; it has a greater range of colour: blues, pinks, mauves and white.

Flowering period—March–April.

Growing conditions—Good, well-drained soil, fairly sunny position. Plant September/October, 1½–2 inches (3–5cm) deep, spacing 4–6 inches (10–15cm).

Propagation—Divide and replant clumps in early autumn.

WINTER ACONITE
(*Eranthis* sp, Ranunculaceae)
Two species are commonly available, both 3–4 inches (7.5–10cm) high, with yellow buttercup-like flowers above a ruff of leaves. *E. hyemalis* is the commonest and earliest flowering, natural-ized in parts of Britain; *E. cilicica* has slightly larger flowers. *E. tubergenii* is a vigorous hybrid between these two species, with named forms that are slightly scented. All do well beneath deciduous trees and shrubs.

Flowering period—*E. hyemalis* late January–February; others March.

Growing conditions—Any well-drained, but moisture-retentive, soil; sun or partial shade. Plant August–September 1–2 inches (2.5–5cm) deep, about 3 inches (7.5cm) apart.

Propagation—Lift and divide tubers as the plants begin to die down; replant.

CHAPTER 6
HERBACEOUS PERENNIALS

Herbaceous perennials are plants which go on from year to year, dying down every winter and producing new stems and leaves in the spring. Some leave no trace on the surface during their dormant period, whereas others keep just a low covering of leaves. A few useful plants are almost 'evergreen', although there is no permanent woody framework as there is with shrubs; examples are London pride (*Saxifraga*) and bergenias.

A perennial plant can be defined strictly as one which lives for three or more years. Short-lived perennials such as aquilegias, coreopsis, delphiniums and lupins are best raised afresh from seed every three or four years, but most herbaceous plants have a much longer life. They do, however, need lifting, dividing and replanting to keep them from deteriorating (see page 79); this is also a good way to increase your stock. The exceptions are few but, for example, hellebores and Japanese anemones (*Anemone × hybrida*) are two that flourish best if left undisturbed.

Using herbaceous perennials in the garden

Most herbaceous perennials are only interesting in summer, but during this time they can provide outstanding colour in almost any situation from a small corner to a long border. However, in most situations it is better to combine them with shrubs and bulbs which give spring and autumn colour (see Chapter 5). The few herbaceous plants which do keep winter leaves are particularly useful in a small garden where you can least afford an empty space.

Wide borders – at least 5 feet (1.5m) across – or 'island' beds surrounded by lawn or paths, show off the range of herbaceous plants to their best advantage. In narrow borders, use only short sturdier varieties (roughly no taller than half the width of the border). Tall plants tend to flop and leave no room for introducing the gradations in height that give a border its attractive form when viewed from a distance. This is particularly pertinent to borders along a wall or solid fence, where plants at the back tend to become drawn.

Never plant right up to a wall, fence or hedge but leave a gap to give your plants some light and air. Reflection of heat from a wall can create an atmosphere which is too hot for some plants, and hedges and shrubs will compete with them for food and moisture. The hedge can also suffer: its lower branches which are shaded in summer make poor growth and look ugly in winter, and its roots are disturbed when the herbaceous plants are lifted and divided. You should thus leave at least 2 feet (0.6m) between most plants and a hedge or large shrub. Bulbs and a few spring flowering shallow-rooted plants like lungwort (*Pulmonaria*) can some-

Table 10: Herbaceous perennials that will grow well in difficult conditions.

Dry and sunny	Dry and shady	Permanently moist
Achillea sp	*Alchemilla mollis*	*Aruncus dioicus*
Alyssum saxatile	*Bergenia* sp	*Astillbe arendsii*
Bergenia sp	*Brunnera* sp	*Caltha palustris*
Centuarea sp	*Euphorbia* sp	*Filipendula ulmaria*
Centranthus ruber	*Geranium macrorrhizum*	*Hosta* sp
Dianthus sp	*Lamium* sp	*Lysimachia* sp
Dictamnus sp	*Liriope muscari*	*Lythrum salicaria*
Echinops sp	*Polygonatum*	*Polygonum* sp
Euphorbia sp		*Primula florindae*
Gypsophila paniculata		*Ranunculus* sp
Iberis sempervirens		*Symphytum* sp
Kniphofia uvaria		*Trollius* sp
Limonium latifolium		
Lychnis sp		
Nepeta sp		
Papaver orientale		
Pulsatilla vulgaris		
Saponaria officinalis		
Sedum sp		
Verbascum sp		

Partial shade and/or dappled shade	Full shade
Ajuga reptans	*Anemone japonica*
Alchemilla mollis	*Euphorbia* sp
Aquilegia sp	*Helleborus* sp
Aruncus dioicus	*Hosta* sp
Astrantia sp	*Polygonatum* × *hybridum*
Bergenia sp	*Symphytum grandiflorum*
Brunnera macrophylla	*Tellima grandiflora*
Campanula sp	
Dicentra sp	
Gallium odoratum	
Geranium sp	
Hemerocallis	
Lamium sp	
Liriope muscari	
Omphaloides sp	
Phlox maculata	
Primula sp	
Pulmonaria sp	
Ranunculus sp	
Tiarella cordifolia	
Trillium sp	
Viola odorata	

times be used to fill in the gap.

Try to establish large clumps of each variety – anything from 18 inches (45cm) to 3 feet (1m) across, depending on the size of the border. Such patches have much more impact than isolated plants. You can gain this effect almost instantly by planting three or four specimens close together, but this can work out expensive if you are buying plants. An alternative is to plant just one or two and help them spread by dividing them annually.

Traditional beds and borders are not the only places where hardy perennials can be used. A few large imposing perennials such as goatsbeard (*Aruncus*) make handsome specimen plants. Those that are vigorous and dense enough to prevent grass coming through can be grown amongst large shrubs in 'wild' roughly mown areas. Primroses (*Primula*) can actually be mown over, provided that the blades are set high and mowing is not begun until late July. Comfrey (*Symphytum*) and yellow archangel (*Lamium galeobdolon*) will cover large areas instead of grass but both can become invasive. Shade-tolerant plants such as *Geranium macrorrhizum*, dead nettle (*Lamium maculatum*) and bugle (*Ajuga*) can be grown under shrubs in wild areas, as here there is little competition from grass.

Growing conditions

Most herbaceous perennials like a reasonably good well-drained soil. A poor or heavy soil can usually be improved sufficiently to grow them by digging in plenty of organic matter (see Chapter 2). Given these soil conditions – where moisture is retained but without waterlogging – most of them thrive best in sunshine. Some of the taller and/or flimsier plants will also need a sheltered position. Some examples of plants that need or will tolerate

different conditions are given in Table 10.

Most are not fussy as to whether the soil is acid or alkaline. However, there are a few exceptions: gentians only grow well in an acid soil, and dianthus and scabious prefer a limy one.

All-season colour

The majority of herbaceous perennials bloom for only a few weeks during the period from June to September. The challenge is to obtain continuity of colour by planting different varieties that will be in flower at different times. There are also a few with which you can extend the season: for example, hellebores and primulas in spring; Japanese anemones and Michaelmas daisies (*Aster* sp) in autumn. More ideas are given in Table 11. The value of a plant can, of course, extend beyond its flowering period if it has attractive foliage: aquilegias, astilbes, bergenias and sedums are notable examples.

In the main flowering period, you have to decide whether you prefer a mixture of different colours or just a few shades which harmonize. Some grand gardens have whole 'mini-gardens' containing plants of just one or two colours, and this is very striking. You can adapt the idea to a small garden, but it does put yet another constraint on your choice of plants.

Scent

Relatively few herbaceous plants have scented flowers, but those that do are worth seeking out.

Hardy border carnations (*Dianthus* hybrids) are famous for their clove-like scent (look for names like 'Perfect Clove' in the catalogues). The closely related garden pinks need less care and the 'old-fashioned' varieties such as 'Mrs Sinkins', 'Charles Musgrave' and 'White Ladies' which are still

Table 11: Herbaceous perennials which bloom outside the main summer period.

Early spring	Late spring	Early summer	Autumn
Bergenia sp	*Brunnera macrophylla*	*Achillea* sp	*Anemone* × *hybrida*
Helleborus niger	*Caltha palustris*	*Ajuga reptans*	*Aster* sp
Primula sp	*Dicentra* sp	*Aquilegia* sp	*Chrysanthemum*
Viola odorata	*Euphorbia* sp	*Astrantia* sp	*rebellum*
	Helleborus orientalis	*Incarvillea delavayi*	*Echinacea purpurea*
	Pulmonaria sp	*Lamium maculatum*	*Liriope muscari*
	Pulsatilla vulgaris	*Lupinus* hybrids	*Polygonum affine*
		Nepeta mussinii	*Schizostylis coccinea*
		Omphalodes cappadocica	*Sedum spectabile*
		Paeonia officinalis	*Solidago* sp
		Papaver orientale	*Viola odorata*
		Polygonatum ×	
		hybridum	
		Tiarella cordifolia	
		Trollius × *hybridus*	

available have a characteristic sweet scent; a few 'modern pink' (*Dianthus* × *allwoodii*) varieties such as 'Doris' are also scented. The sweet violet (*Viola odorata*) is another perfumed plant that has lost its popularity – in favour of the larger-flowered pansies – but it can still be obtained.

Unlike the common early flowering peonies (*Paeonia officinalis*), many of the June-flowering Chinese peonies (*Paeonia lactiflora*) are strongly scented: try varieties such as 'Duchesse de Nemours' and 'Sarah Bernhardt'. Border phlox are also fragrant; even the modern vibrant orange/red colours.

Cutting

Many herbaceous perennials survive well in water and provide a wide choice for summer displays, but a few are worth a special mention.

Christmas and Lenten roses (*Helleborus*), unexpectedly for spring flowers, hold their large blooms in perfect condition indoors provided they have 'set': do not pick them while the stamens are still heavy with pollen.

Shasta daisies (*Chrysanthemum maximum*) are like the proper florists' chrysanthemums in that they make a foolproof, lasting display. Asters and rudbeckia have similar qualities.

The perennial gypsophila provides billowy clouds of white or pale pink flowers, ideal for setting off bright, solid blooms. Lady's mantle (*Alchemilla*) has frothy yellow-green flowerheads, useful in similar ways. Compared with annuals, there are few perennial flowers which are good for drying. Everlasting pearl (*Anaphalis*) is one that is popular. The flowerheads of yarrow (the gold, not pink, forms), globe thistles (*Echinops*) and sea holly (*Eryngium*) can also be used.

In the past, the flowers of primroses, cowslips and violets were picked from the hedgerows to decorate salads and sweets, but it is hard to sacrifice blooms from the garden for such a purpose! One attractive border plant valuable for its culinary use is red bergamot (*Monarda didyma*). The petals can be added to salad and the leaves make a delicate tea very like a fine China tea.

Wildlife

Herbaceous plants can be good sources of pollen and nectar for insects. As with annuals and bulbs, you should choose single rather than double varieties and include some of the old cottage garden flowers which are closely related to native species.

Summer flowers popular with bees include campanulas, scabious, sea lavender (*Limonium*), perennial cornflowers (*Centaurea*), catmint (*Nepeta*) and bugle (*Ajuga*). In autumn, Michaelmas daisies are a mainstay. Butterflies also visit most of these plants, but they find two others especially attractive: these are red valerian (*Centranthus ruber*), often seen growing from old walls, and the iceplant (*Sedum spectabile*); choose the common species rather than named varieties or hybrids which have a different flower colour. Flowers easily accessible to hoverflies include yarrow (*Achillea*), Shasta daisies (*Chrysanthemum maximum*), rudbeckia, and golden rod (*Solidago*).

Seedheads left on in autumn provide food for birds and need not necessarily be an eyesore: those of yarrow, astilbe, golden rod, and globe thistles are quite attractive.

Some native herbaceous plants can make attractive garden plants, provided you give them a suitable position; examples are given in Table 12.

Table 12: Native herbaceous perennials that can make attractive garden plants.

Ajuga reptans (bugle)
Caltha palustris (marsh marigold)
Geranium pratense (meadow crane's-bill)
Polygonatum × *hybridum* (Solomon's seal)
Primula vulgaris (primrose)
Primula veris (cowslip)
Pulsatilla vulgaris (pasque flower)
Thalictrum flavum (meadow rue)

Buying seeds and plants

Seeds

Many herbaceous perennials can be grown from seed and most of the major seed companies sell between 50 and 100 varieties – a few up to 200. There is thus a large range to choose from and this includes some varieties that are often hard to find as plants (verbascums, for example).

Raising your own plants in this way is very much cheaper than buying them – a great advantage if you are planning a new garden. You can afford to plant in large groups, which will quickly give the beds and borders an established look. There is also far less danger of introducing disease into the garden. Plants such as lupins and aquilegias which give a mixed colour range are particularly good value.

Against this is the fact that some good plants cannot be grown from seed, either because their seed is not viable or because they are selected varieties which do not come true from seed. You are most likely to be successful with plants whose garden forms are closely related to the wild species. Another disadvantage is that it can take three or four years for plants to reach flowering size (hellebores, for example, are very slow); however, two years is the average time.

Table 13 lists a few easy-to-grow plants and gives a few warnings: germination is not always as infallible as the instructions on the seed packet imply. For further information about sowing methods see Chapter 3.

Plants

Although garden centres offer a considerable choice of plants, these will not necessarily be the most worthwhile varieties to grow. Before you make a purchase, read the labels carefully and

Table 13: Herbaceous perennials from seed: varieties easily obtainable.

Easy to grow plants	Comment
Achillea sp	Also easy to propagate by division.
Aquilegia sp	Short-lived and not easy to divide.
Campanula sp	Plants may be variable.
Chrysanthemum maximum	Plants may be variable.
Coreopsis grandiflora	Will flower first year if sown early.
Dianthus sp	
Dorinicum sp	
Echinops ritro	Also easy to divide.
Geum chiloense	
Gypsophila paniculata	Short-lived and not easy to divide.
Incarvillea delavayi	
Linum sp	
Lupinus hybrids	Good variety of colours – chip seed coat.
Lychnis sp	
Nepeta mussinii	Lots of plants may be required for edging.
Papaver orientale	
Verbascum phoeniceum	Short-lived; plants not easily bought.

Problem plants	Comment
Alstroemeria	Mature plants resent disturbance, so seed worth trying, but difficult to germinate.
Delphinium	Germination of bought seed may be poor.
Eryngium	Germination may be slow and erratic.
Helleborus niger	Seed needs frost treatment and germination is slow and erratic.
Trollius × *hybridus*	Germination may be slow and erratic.

check that the plant is really suitable for your garden – never buy one that is *not* properly labelled. Most are 'container-grown': that is, they are sold in polythene or rigid plastic pots. The plant roots should be spread throughout the compost in the pot, but it should not be pot bound or starved of nutrients. Tell-tale signs are yellowing, wilting leaves and lots of roots growing from the bottom of the container. And, of course, avoid any plants showing signs of pest or disease attack.

In spring and autumn, you may find dormant bare-rooted plants on sale – particularly in high street shops. These are packaged in polythene bags and have moist moss or compost around their roots. They are cheaper than containerized plants, but there will be little choice of variety. If you do find something you like, make sure it has *not* started to sprout in the warmth of the shop and that the roots look healthy.

For the greatest range of varieties you will need to visit a specialist nursery or order from them by post. The fact that particular varieties are not popularly on sale in garden centres does not mean that they are difficult to grow: it is often quite the opposite. However, even if one of the nursery catalogues lists the plants you are looking for, you must be prepared for a few to be out of stock (give alternatives on the order form if possible). Plants are usually posted in

Containerized plants

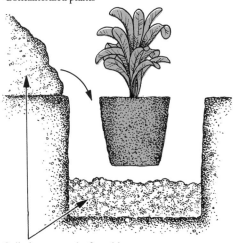

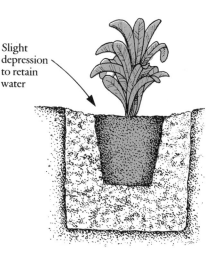

Slight
depression
to retain
water

Soil plus peat or leafmould

1 Water the plant well. Dig a hole
larger than the pot and mix peat
or leafmould into the bottom of
the hole. Tip the plant from its pot
without disturbing the root ball.

2 Fill in the space with top soil mixed with peat,
firming it gently. Water the plant well.

Bare-rooted plants

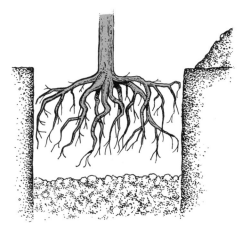

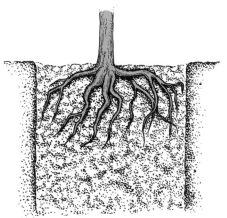

1 Dig a hole large enough to spread the
roots right out, and mix peat or leafmould into
the bottom. Set the plant in the hole at the
correct depth, spreading the roots out and down.

2 Fill in soil/peat mixture around them,
shaking the plant gently, to make sure
there are no air pockets. Fill in the rest of the
mixture, firming it well.

Figure 20. Planting herbaceous perennials.

polythene with their roots surrounded by damp newspaper, straw or peat. Unpack them as soon as they arrive and if you cannot plant them out immediately, keep them in a frost-free place with their roots moist.

Planting

When to plant
Perennial plants bought in containers can be set out at any time, provided they are kept well watered. The best time for planting bare-rooted plants is in early spring, but in places where the weather is not too severe it can be done in the autumn or during mild spells in winter.

Spacing
This depends very much on the situation and the size of the plants. Some idea of the height and spread of individual varieties is given in the last section of this chapter. Ideally, clumps in a border should be spaced so that no bare earth is visible between them during the summer, but so that they do not swamp neighbouring plants. Spacing is best judged by experience and can be adjusted as you lift and divide the plants or let them spread. As a rough guide, allow about 1 foot (0.3m) between low clumps and 2 feet (0.6m) between tall ones.

Planting methods
Give the plants a good start by helping the roots spread into the surrounding soil: dig a large planting hole and use peat or leafmould as shown in Figure 20. The plants should be set in to the same depth as they were previously growing. This is easy to judge with containerized plants, but you should also be able to see a soil mark on the old stems of bare-rooted ones. Keep the plants well watered if the weather is dry.

After care
A well-planted herbaceous bed needs surprisingly little regular attention.

Weeding
In spring, weed between plants and, if possible, apply a mulch of well-rotted compost or manure. This prevents annual weeds from germinating and keeps the soil moist. In an established border the plants should grow up and cover the ground so that ideally there is no need to weed during the summer. Some perennial weeds will still persist, however. Bindweed is one of the worst problems: with its roots amongst the plant roots, it climbs up the flimsiest of stems and is impossible to weed out without damage. The only real solution is to make sure there are no such weeds in the ground before you plant (see Chapter 2) and pull up any small new shoots as they appear.

Table 14: Herbaceous perennials over 1 foot (30cm) tall that usually do not need supporting.

Achillea	Limonium
(short varieties)	Liriope
Alchemilla	Lychnis
Anchusa	Lysimachia
Asters (dwarf)	Lythrum
Astilbe	Nepeta
Brunnera	Omphalodes
Campanula	Phlox
(short varieties)	Polemonium
Centurea	Polygonum
Centranthus	Potentilla
Dicentra	Pulmonaria
Echinops	Salvia
Euphorbia	Scabious
Filipendula	Schizostylis
Geranium	Sedum
Geum	Senecio
Hellebore	Solidago
Hemerocallis	Trollius
Kniphofia	Verbascum
Litris	

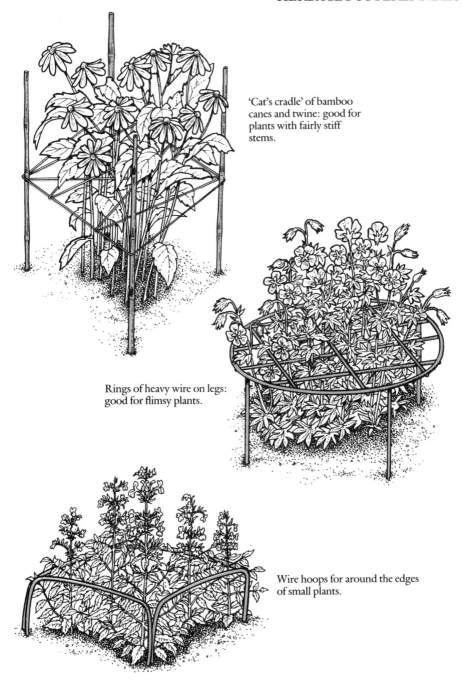

'Cat's cradle' of bamboo canes and twine: good for plants with fairly stiff stems.

Rings of heavy wire on legs: good for flimsy plants.

Wire hoops for around the edges of small plants.

Figure 21. Supporting herbaceous perennials.

Staking

Tall plants will often need support, especially in exposed gardens. However, putting in stakes can take a lot of time and rarely looks completely natural, so it is worth avoiding them where possible.

The chief way of doing this is to grow plants which are self-supporting: either because they are naturally sturdy or because they naturally sprawl without detriment to their looks! A list of such plants is given in Table 14. It is those that are 'top heavy', often because they have been bred to give large flowers, that are most vulnerable. Those under 1 foot (0.3m) tall rarely need any support. All plants are likely to be sturdier if grown in the right conditions – with plenty of light and a balanced 'diet'. You can also use shrubs to provide shelter and support.

Any staking that is necessary should be done early, before the plant grows up: hasty summer remedies to shore up flopping foliage nearly always look ugly. You can use pea sticks as for annuals (see Figure 15), bamboo canes and string, or some of the purpose-made wire and plastic supports available (Figure 21).

Watering

Most herbaceous plants benefit from watering during long dry spells: wilting phlox are a good 'drought indicator' as these quickly show signs of stress. Water thoroughly once with a hose rather than giving the plants continual light sprinklings, as these can encourage fungal diseases.

Dead-heading

Removing faded blooms from early summer flowers such as lupins, phlox and delphiniums encourages fresh growth and sometimes a second crop of flowers. From late autumn onwards, untidy dead growth can be cut off to ground level. Remember, however, that birds will enjoy large seedheads and that dry stems provide welcome shelter for overwintering insects like ladybirds, so there is an excuse for not being too spick and span. Old growth can also help protect the crowns of less hardy plants in very cold weather.

Dividing and replanting

After three or four years, clumps of most herbaceous plants tend to become tatty and flower less freely. This is because the roots and stems at the centre of the clump become starved and weakened, while those on the outside thrive in fresh soil. It is then time to lift and divide the clumps, replanting the young vigorous parts and discarding the old centre (see Chapter 3). Summer-flowering plants should generally be divided in autumn, but in cold places early spring is the best time to split late flowering plants, and early summer is best for spring flowers such as primroses. Although this may seem a lot of unnecessary work, the plants will look much better and need less care the following season. There are a few exceptions, however: peonies and Japanese anemones, for example, are slow to establish and should be left undisturbed once planted. Gypsophila and incarvillea are difficult to divide successfully.

Pests and diseases

Herbaceous perennials have few troubles that they cannot overcome by vigorous growth. Thus soil preparation, mulching, dividing and – above all – choosing the right position for the plant minimize the effects of common garden pests and diseases. Details of these and their control are given in Chapter 2, but there are some particular hazards to look out for with herbaceous plants.

Soil pests such as leather jackets, cutworms and wireworms should not be damaging to established plants, but some are susceptible to eelworm – most commonly phlox, gypsophila and primulas. Slugs and snails are always a danger to young shoots in spring, particularly the sappy growth of delphiniums, lupins and primulas. Make sure there is no debris around the plants by this time. Slugs and other leaf-eating creatures such as caterpillars are rarely a problem once the plants are full grown. Aphids are, similarly, most harmful to young shoots and many herbaceous perennials are not susceptible, although there are exceptions. There is an enormous light green aphid which attacks lupins: each looks twice the size of an ordinary greenfly and must make quite a meal for any ladybird!

Powdery mildew is the disease most likely to be seen in herbaceous plants – covering the leaves, stems, and sometimes even the flowers, with a white powdery coat. Michaelmas daisies, delphiniums, golden rod and phlox are particularly susceptible, but it can help to choose your varieties carefully. For example *Aster frikartii* is far less prone to mildew than true Michaelmas daisies (*Aster novae-angliae* and *Aster novi-belgii*).

Other diseases crop up with less regularity, but can be troublesome when they do occur. Virus disease is always a possibility, but is often connected with lupins, delphiniums and primulas; similarly, leaf spot (often seen on hellebores) and leaf miners (common on Shasta daisies) can attack any plant.

A selection of herbaceous perennials

ASTERS/MICHAELMAS DAISIES
(*Aster* sp, Compositae)
All asters have daisy-like flowers on stiff stems; usually they have yellow centres although some varieties are almost double. They come in white and many shades of purple, blue, pink and red. *A. novae-angliae* and *A. novi-belgii* are the true Michaelmas daisies; tall varieties 2–5 feet (60cm–1.5m), planting distance 15 inches (38cm), usually need staking and most are prone to mildew; dwarf varieties around 1 foot (30cm) are less trouble. *A. amellus* and *A.* × *frikartii* varieties are easier to grow and far less prone to mildew, although the colour range is more limited. Asters are useful lasting late-flowering border plants, loved by bees and excellent for cutting.

Flowering period—*A. amellus* August–September; others August–October.

Growing conditions—Rich moist soils are best, especially for Michaelmas daisies, which should also be divided annually to avoid overcrowding. Sunny position.

Propagation—Divide clumps during October–March.

Diseases—Many varieties are susceptible to powdery mildew; *A. novi-belgii* varieties are sometimes affected by wilt.

BERGAMOT
(*Monarda didyma*, Labiatae)
Bushy plants, height 2–3 feet (60–90cm), spacing 2 feet (60cm), with whorls of flowers – commonly red, but named hybrids also come in shades of pink and mauve. A good border plant, loved by bees and butterflies; the aromatic foliage of the common species makes a delicate flavoured tea and the dried flowers are good in pot-pourri.

Flowering period—June–September.

Growing conditions—A moist soil containing plenty of compost is essential; sun or partial shade. Water and mulch in hot spells.

Propagation—Divide clumps in autumn or spring. The species can be grown from seed sown indoors in March.

BERGENIA
(*Bergenia* sp, Saxifragaceae)
The garden species and named hybrids all have large rounded leathery leaves, forming green mounds about 9–12 inches (23–30cm) high which remain throughout the winter; planting distance 18 inches (45cm). Colour of the flower spikes ranges from pale pink (*B. crassifolia*), deep pink (*B. cordifolia*) to purple red (*B. purpurascens*). The leaves often take a reddish tinge in autumn. A very useful early flowering plant for the front of borders.

Flowering period—*B. cordifolia* and *B. crassifolia* March–April; *B. purpurascens* April–May.

Growing conditions—Almost all types of soil; sun or partial shade.

Propagation—Divide overcrowded clumps in autumn.

Diseases—Sometimes suffers from leaf spot.

BISTORT
(*Polygonum bistorta*, Polygonaceae)
A native species, the main garden variety being 'Superbum', height up to 3 feet (1m), planting distance 2 feet (60cm). Bright pink 'bottle brush' flowerheads come on stems above a dense mat of foliage. A useful early hardy border plant.

Flowering period—May–June.

Growing conditions—Rich moist soil is preferable, but any reasonable soil will do; sun or partial shade.

Propagation—Divide clumps in autumn or spring.

CATMINT
(*Nepeta* × *faassenii, N. mussinii*, Labiatae)
A bushy plant with grey-green leaves and lavender blue flowers; height 12–18 inches (30–45cm), spacing 12 inches (30cm). Taller named varieties are sometimes available and *N. nervosa* is more compact with greener leaves. A good plant for the front of the border; a favourite with bees.

Flowering period—May–September.

Growing conditions—Any well-drained garden soil; sunny position. Tall varieties need staking.

Propagation—Divide established clumps in early spring or take basal cuttings. *N. nervosa* can be grown from seed sown inside in March or April.

CHRYSANTHEMUMS
(Shasta daisies and Korean chrysanthemums)
(*Chrysanthemum* sp, Compositae)
Unlike the florists' chrysanthemums, these border chrysanthemums are hardy. *C. maximum* (Shasta daisy) height 2½–3 feet (60–90cm), spacing 12–18 inches (30–45cm) has large white daisy-like flowers, although many named varieties are double. *C. rubellum* (Korean chrysanthemum), height 1½–2½ feet (45–75cm) has flowers in shades of pink or yellow depending on variety; a useful late-flowering plant. All varieties are excellent for cutting.

Flowering period—*C. maximum* June–August; *C. rubellum* August–October.

Growing conditions—Most soils are adequate but one that is fertile, well-drained and alkaline is preferable. Lift and divide clumps every three years. Plants will need staking in exposed positions.

Propagation—Lift and divide established clumps or take basal cuttings in March and April.

Pests—Can be affected by eelworm and leaf miners.

Diseases—Leaf spot may cause circular black or brown spots. Occasionally affected by rust.

COLUMBINE
(*Aquilegia vulgaris*, Ranunculaceae)
A short-lived plant with delicate grey green leaves and 'granny's bonnet'

flowers on long wiry stems. Height 18 inches–3 feet (45cm–1m), spacing 1 foot (30cm). The original species has relatively small blue, pink or white flowers with short spurs. Many catalogues now only list the new hybrids which have larger long-spurred flowers in a wider mix of colours. A traditional cottage garden plant, but useful in formal borders because of its early flowering and attractive foliage.

Flowering period—May–June.

Growing conditions—Any well-drained soil containing some organic matter; sun or partial shade.

Propagation—Sow seeds in March in pots in a cool greenhouse or May–July outdoors; readily self-seeds.

Pests—A species of leaf miner tunnels the leaves, but it is not common.

Diseases—Occasionally subject to leaf spot and rust.

COMFREY
(*Symphytum* sp, Boraginaceae)
The native comfrey S. *officinalis* (white, pink or mauve flowers) and Russian comfrey S. × *uplandicum* (blue-purple flowers) are vigorous plants growing up to 3 feet (1m) or more; best in wild areas. S. *caucasium*, height 2 feet (60cm), planting distance 18 inches (45cm), has bright blue flowers and can be used in borders. S. *grandiflorum*, height 8 inches (20cm), planting distance 15 inches (38cm) has creamy white flowers; it is a spreading plant useful under trees and shrubs, and in dark corners.

Flowering period—S. *grandiflorum* April–May; others May–August.

Growing conditions—Any reasonable soil, although best in rich moist conditions; sun or shade.

Propagation—Divide clumps in spring, autumn or winter, or take root cuttings.

Diseases—Rust is sometimes a problem.

CRANE'SBILL
(*Geranium* sp, Geraniaceae)
Many of these species and their hybrids are useful border plants (not to be confused with the pot and bedding 'geraniums' which are botanically 'pelargoniums'). *G. pratense* (the native meadow crane's-bill) has attractive floppy foliage forming a dense mound about 18 inches (45cm) high, planting distance 2 feet (60cm). The flowers are saucer shaped, commonly deep blue but there are named varieties in white and other shades of blue, some with double flowers. 'Johnson's blue' is a popular hybrid. *G. macrorrhizum*, height 1 foot (30cm), planting distance 15 inches (38cm) is a more spreading plant with pink flowers; useful for growing amongst shrubs.

Flowering period—*G. macrorrhizum* May–June; *G. pratense* June–August.

Growing conditions—Any ordinary soil. *G. pratense* will grow in sun or light shade. *G. macrorrhizum* is more shade tolerant and can withstand dry conditions.

Propagation—Divide clumps between September and March.

DAY LILY
(*Hemerocallis* sp, Liliaceae)
There are many named garden hybrids. All have wide grassy leaves and large trumpet-shaped flowers formed up stiff stems. Height 2–3 feet (60–90cm), planting distance 18 inches (45cm). Flowers come in many shades of yellow, orange, pink and red. Each individual flower is short lived, but new ones constantly appear on the same stems. Provides good contrast in a mixed or herbaceous border.

Flowering period—June–August depending on variety.

Growing conditions—Good soil preferable; sun or light shade.

Propagation—Divide clumps between October and April.

EVERLASTING PEA
(*Lathyrus latifolius*, Leguminosae)
A climber, height 6 feet (2m), planting distance 18 inches (45cm), similar to annual sweet peas, but the flowers are small on short stems in shades of white, pink, red and violet. An old cottage garden plant, which can be trained against a fence or allowed to ramble amongst tall shrubs.

Flowering period—June–September.

Growing conditions—Fertile, well-drained soil; sunny position.

Propagation—Sow seeds in March–April in pots in a greenhouse, soaking them first to speed up germination. Alternatively, divide roots in March.

GARDEN PINKS
(*Dianthus* sp, Caryophyllaceae)
All pinks have tufts of grey-green leaves, remaining all winter, with flowers on stiff stems. Height 10–15 inches (25–38cm), spacing 9–12 inches (25–30cm). Old-fashioned pinks are hybrids derived from a wild European pink. They have only one flush of flowers; these are single or double, white or pink, sometimes marked with darker colours; they are very fragrant. Modern pinks (*D.* × *allwoodii*) are hybrids derived from crossing old-fashioned pinks with border carnations; they grow more quickly and bloom over a longer period, but not all are as fragrant as the old varieties. They are excellent edging and border plants because of their neat, lasting foliage. Dwarf hybrids, height 3–6 inches (7–15cm) are good for containers, walls and rock gardens.

Flowering period—Old-fashioned pinks – June; modern pinks – mostly in June/July and again in September/October.

Growing conditions—Any ordinary well-drained soil, preferably not acid; a sunny spot is essential. Tolerates dry conditions.

Propagation—Take cuttings June–August and root in a shaded cold frame if possible. The plants are short-lived, especially modern pinks, and should be replaced every few years.

Diseases—Leaf spot can cause brown or white spots with purple margins.

HELLEBORES
(Christmas and Lenten roses and Stinking hellebores)
(*Helleborus* sp, Ranunculaceae)
The Christmas rose (*H. niger*), height 12–18 inches (30–45cm), spacing 18 inches (45cm) has dark evergreen leaves and large white open flowers with gold stamens. The Lenten rose (*H. orientalis*), height 18–24 inches (45–60cm), evergreen in mild winters, has flowers in shades of purple, pink and white. The native stinking hellebore (*H. foetidus*), height and planting distance 24 inches (60cm), evergreen, has many smaller light green cupped flowers. They are all good plants for mixed borders because of their evergreen foliage and early long-lasting flowers; also useful for flower arrangements.

Flowering period—*H. niger* January–March, *H. orientalis* and *H. foetidus* February–April.

Growing conditions—Deep well-drained but moist soils are best, but will often grow well in heavy clay; partially shaded position. Dislikes disturbance.

Propagation—Not easy to grow from seed; sow in pots in midsummer and overwinter in a cold frame. Divide plants of Christmas or Lenten roses in March.

Diseases—Leaf spot may cause elliptical black blotches.

ICE PLANT
(*Sedum* sp, Crassulaceae)
The border sedums have fleshy leaves and wide flat heads of tiny flowers; height 1–2 feet (30–60cm), planting

distance 18 inches (45cm). *S. spectabile* has grey-green leaves and pink flower-heads and is the form most attractive to butterflies. *S. telephium*, a native species, has a garden form 'Munstead red' with dark red flowers. The popular 'Autumn joy' is a hybrid between these two species and has rose-red flowers. *S. maximum purpureum* has grey-purple leaves and dusky red flowers. All varieties are useful for their attractive foliage and late flowers.

Flowering period—August–October.

Growing conditions—Well-drained soil (tolerant of dry conditions); sunny position.

Propagation—Divide clumps October–March or take basal cuttings in late spring.

Diseases—Root rot can occur in wet soil.

JAPANESE ANEMONE

(*Anemone × hybrida A. japonica*, Ranunculaceae)
There are many named forms, heights from 1½–3 feet (45–90cm), planting distance 12–18 inches (30–45cm), with attractive vine-like leaves and pink or white open flowers on stiff stems. Good late-flowering border plants.

Flowering period—August–October.

Growing conditions—A good well-drained soil is best; sun or partial shade. It is deep-rooted – slow to establish but later can be invasive. Leave undisturbed for several years after planting.

Propagation—Divide clumps between October and March, or take root cuttings between November and January.

LADY'S MANTLE

(*Alchemilla mollis*, Rosaceae)
Rounded light green leaves form a mound about 1 foot (30cm) high, spread 18 inches (45cm), from which

arise frothy sprays of tiny greenish yellow flowers. An excellent plant for the front of the border; invaluable for flower arranging.

Flowering period—June–August.

Growing conditions—Any well-drained garden soil, preferably with some compost added; sun or partial shade. Prune away the old growth in September.

Propagation—Sow seed outdoors in March or April, or divide established clumps October–March. Readily self-seeds.

LEOPARD'S BANE

(*Doronicum* sp, Compositae)
Most named varieties are of *D. planta-gineum*; heights vary from 1–3 feet (30–90cm), planting distance 12–18 inches (30–45cm). They have heart-shaped leaves and large yellow daisy-like flowers on stiff stems. A useful early border plant; good for cutting.

Flowering period—April–June.

Growing conditions—Moist soil, sun or partial shade. Tall plants may need staking.

Propagation—Divide clumps between October and March.

LONDON PRIDE

(*Saxifraga × urbium*, Saxifragaceae)
Low rosettes of fleshy leaves cover the ground all year round; sprays of pink flowers in summer; height and planting distance 1 foot (30cm). A similar type (*S. umbrosa primuloides*) has deep pink flowers. Useful for edging.

Flowering period—May–June.

Growing conditions—A soil rich in organic matter is best; sun or partial shade.

Propagation—Divide clumps in autumn or detach non-flowering rosettes in early summer and treat them as cuttings.

LUNGWORT

(*Pulmonaria* sp, Boraginaceae)
P. officinalis is the common lungwort, height and spacing 1 foot (30cm), familiar for its white spotted leaves and pink flowers fading to blue. *P. angustifolia* has unspotted leaves, and there are named garden varieties with blue or pink flowers. *P. saccharata* has striking silver-spotted leaves and pink-blue flowers. All are useful early flowering plants for planting under trees and shrubs; they spread quickly.

Flowering period—April–May.

Growing conditions—Moist soil containing plenty of organic matter is preferable, but will grow in most soils in a shady position.

Propagation—Divide clumps in autumn.

MASTERWORT

(*Astrantia* sp, Umbelliferae)
The species commonly available are all similar, forming clumps 18–24 inches (45–60cm) high, planting distance 12–15 inches (30–38cm). The flowerheads consist of starry flowers of greenish or pinkish white, surrounded by bracts of similar colour. They are not showy, but are lasting and blend well into a mixed border. Good for cutting and can be dried.

Flowering period—June–August.

Growing conditions—A moist soil is best, but most soils are adequate; partially shaded position.

Propagation—Divide clumps between October and March. Sow seeds in pots in September and overwinter in a greenhouse or cold frame.

MEADOWSWEET/DROPWORT

(*Filipendula* sp, Rosaceae)
F. ulmaria (meadowsweet) and *F. vulgaris* (dropwort) are both native plants, height 2–3 feet (60–90cm), spacing 18 inches (45cm). *F. vulgaris* has fern-like leaves and fluffy heads of tiny flowers on long stems; they are creamy white, sometimes tinged with pink. *F. ulmaria* also has deeply cut leaves; flower sprays are creamy white; the variety 'Aurea' has yellowy leaves.

Flowering period—June–July.

Growing conditions—*F. ulmaria* needs moist soil and partial shade; *F. vulgaris* needs less moisture and will grow in sun or shade.

Propagation—Divide clumps in spring or autumn.

MULLEIN

(*Verbascum* sp, Scrophulariaceae)
The native mullein is a biennial *V. thapsus* which has a rosette of woolly grey leaves and yellow flowers on spikes up to 3 feet (1m) high, planting distance 12 inches (30cm). Most garden forms are short-lived perennial hybrids, *V. hybridum*; they have flowering spikes anything from 2–6 feet (0.6–2m) high depending on variety, in shades of yellow, pink, maroon and orange. A good plant for dry places – shorter varieties will grow up between paving and at the base of walls.

Flowering period—June–August.

Growing conditions—Well-drained soil which is not too rich; full sun.

Propagation—Sow seeds in April in a nursery bed or pots outdoors; take root cuttings in February or March.

Pests—The yellow, black and green mullein moth caterpillar often attacks the leaves.

PASQUE FLOWER

(*Pulsatilla vulgaris*, Ranunculaceae)
A native downland plant with soft ferny leaves; height 12 inches (30cm), spacing 15 inches (38cm). Large anemone-like purple flowers with gold centres, followed by feathery seedheads.

Flowering period—April–May.

Growing conditions—A well-drained

soil and open sunny position are essential. They resent disturbance once established.

Propagation—Sow fresh seeds in July and overwinter in cold frame or greenhouse. Plant out in the autumn of the following year.

PRIMROSE and POLYANTHUS

(*Primula vulgaris* and hybrids, Primulaceae)

The wild primrose, height 6 inches (15cm), planting distance 9 inches (23cm), has delicate yellow flowers; garden varieties have a range of colours including blues and reds. Polyanthus – derived from the primrose and the cowslip (*P. veris*) – are usually slightly larger and have bright flowers in clusters on stiff stems; many garden varieties are available, in single colours or mixtures of blues, yellows and reds, but a few (like the 'Pacific' strains) are not reliably hardy. Useful in borders, wild areas and in troughs and pots.

Flowering period—March–May.

Growing conditions—Reasonably fertile, moist soil; partial shade in summer.

Propagation—Sow seeds in pots in May–July or in heat January–March; they may need frost treatment and can be slow and erratic to germinate. Divide established clumps in early summer after flowering.

Pests—Vine weevils and cutworms can cause collapse of plants.

Diseases—Leaf spot can attack plants in poor conditions.

SALVIA

(*Salvia nemorosa, S. superba*, Labiatae)

This is the hardiest of the herbaceous salvias: a stiff bushy plant growing up to 2½ feet (75cm), planting distance 18 inches (45cm), although there are newer more compact forms. The flowers are deep violet blue, loved by bees. A good border plant.

Flowering period—July–September.

Growing conditions—Well-drained soil, with compost added if it is light. Sunny position.

Propagation—Divide clumps between October and March.

SOLOMON'S SEAL

(*Polygonatum* × *hybridum, P. multiflorum*, Liliaceae)

A native plant with attractive arching stems, from which hang white and green tubular flowers. Height 2–3 feet (60–90cm), planting distance 12–18 inches (30–45cm). Grows well amongst trees or shrubs in a mixed border or wild part of the garden. Good for flower arrangements.

Flowering period—May–June.

Growing conditions—Almost any soil, but add compost, peat or leafmould in a dry place; shady position.

Propagation—Divide the spreading roots in autumn or spring.

Pests—Sawfly caterpillars can strip leaves if not spotted in their early stages.

SWEET ROCKET

(*Hesperis matronalis*, Cruciferae)

A short-lived perennial, height generally 2–3 feet (60–90cm), spacing 18 inches (45cm), but there is a dwarf form 'Candidissima', 15 inches (38cm) high. The white or purple flowers carried on long spikes give off a strong sweet scent. A favourite cottage garden or wild garden plant.

Flowering period—June.

Growing conditions—Light, but moist, soil; sunny position.

Propagation—Sow seeds in April or May outdoors, in a nursery bed or pots. Frequently self-seeds.

SWEET VIOLET

(*Viola odorata*, Violaceae)

A native species, still with a place in the garden; height 4–6 inches (10–15cm), spreads by runners over a distance of 1 foot (30cm) or more. Small sweet-smelling flowers, commonly blue or white, but named garden varieties have a wider colour range. Good under trees and shrubs in formal or wild areas, or in borders where summer growth provides some shade.

Flowering period—February–April and sometimes in autumn.

Growing conditions—Moist but well-drained, soil; partial shade.

Propagation—Divide clumps in autumn or take basal cuttings in early summer. Seed needs frost treatment and is slow and erratic to germinate.

VALERIAN
(*Centranthus ruber*, Valerianaceae)
A plant with stiff branched stems about 2 feet (60cm) high; planting distance 18 inches (45cm). The flowerheads consist of clusters of tiny flowers, usually of deep pink, but there are also crimson and white forms. An old cottage garden plant, long flowering and easily grown; one of the best for attracting bees and butterflies.

Flowering period—June–September.

Growing conditions—Thrives in poor, well-drained soil (especially on limestone); sunny places – often seen growing out of walls.

Propagation—Sow seeds in a nursery bed between April and June. Sometimes self-seeds.

YARROW
(*Achilles* sp, Compositae)
Several species make useful border plants. They have ferny foliage and flat flowerheads on long stiff stems. *A. filipendulina* 'Coronation Gold', height 3 feet (1m), planting distance 2 feet (60cm), has deep yellow flowers; *A. millefolium* 'Cerise Queen' (a variety of the native yarrow), height 2½ feet (75cm), planting distance 15 inches (38cm) has deep pink flowers; *A. taygetea* 'Moonshine', height 2 feet (60cm), planting distance 15 inches (38cm), has pale yellow flowers. They attract hoverflies and in winter the heads of golden types make good dried decorations.

Flowering period—June–September.

Growing conditions—Any ordinary well-drained soil (plants will tolerate drought conditions); sunny position; tall varieties may need staking.

Propagation—Divide clumps in spring or autumn. Sow seeds in March or April in pots in a cold greenhouse, or in late spring in a nursery bed.

CHAPTER 7

ROSES

No other family of plants has such a wide range of shapes, sizes, forms and colour as the rose – nor such a complex family tree! The result is a bewildering number of 'classifications', based partly on botany and partly on ancestry, which makes meaningful identification difficult.

The most practical way to group roses is by their appearance and habit – and this is how they should be found in most modern catalogues. The following criteria are used.

Are the roses *modern* or *old* or *wild*?

Old garden roses are cultivated varieties grown before the 1860s when the first modern bush roses were introduced. Wild rose are the natural species or closely related hybrids.

Are they *'recurrent'* or *'non-recurrent'*?

'Recurrent' or 'repeat-flowering' roses bloom continuously over a long period or in more than one significant 'flush'. 'Non-recurrent' roses have only one short flowering period.

Are they *climbing* or *non-climbing*?

Climbing roses have long sprawling or arching stems normally needing support.

The answers to the above questions result in the groups shown on the right of Table 15, which are mostly just 'tidied-up' versions of familiar rose types.

Large-flowered bush roses are the classic rose-bed roses or 'hybrid T's, which bear shapely blooms on long flower stems. They grow between 2½–4 feet (75–120cm) tall and bloom intermittently from mid-summer to mid-autumn.

Cluster-flowered bush roses or 'floribundas' are similar, but have a mass of blooms produced in trusses. They flower almost continuously over the same period as the large-flowered roses; however, the flowers are less 'perfect' and few have more than a faint scent.

Modern shrub roses are large bushy hybrids anything from 4–8 feet (1.2–2.4m) tall. Most – but not all – flower throughout the summer.

Ramblers are vigorous climbing roses with long pliable stems; they usually have one flush of blooms, most of these appearing on the stems produced the previous summer.

Climbers have stiffer stems and the flowers are borne on a more or less permanent framework.

Miniature roses are smaller-scale replicas of the bush or climbing roses, growing only about 18 inches (45cm) high. Most tend to flower best in July and then intermittently until autumn.

Old garden roses are still classified in their original groups based on parentage, although today's catalogues may list only one or two examples in

Table 15: Rose classification.

```
                                                                          ┌ large flowered
                                          ┌ recurrent flowering ┌ shrub              (hybrid tea)
                                          │                     │          bush  ┤ cluster flowered
                          ┌ non-climbing ┤                     └ miniature          (floribunda)
                          │               │                                       └ polyantha
                          │               └ non-recurrent      { shrub
                          │                 flowering
  ┌ modern garden        ┤                                                         ┌ rambler
  │   roses              │               ┌ recurrent flowering                    ┤ climber
  │                      │               │                                         └ climbing miniature
  │                      └ climbing      ┤
  │                                      │                                         ┌ rambler
  │                                      └ non-recurrent                          ┤ climber
  │                                        flowering                              └ climbing miniature
  │
  │                                                                               ┌ Alba
  │                                                                               │ Bourbon
  │                                                                               │ Boursault
  │                                                                               │ China
  │                                                                               │ Damask
  │                                                                               │ Gallica
  │                      ┌ non-climbing                                          ┤ Hybrid Perpetual
  │                      │                                                        │ Moss
  ┤ old garden          │                                                        │ Portland
  │   roses             ┤                                                        │ Provence
  │                      │                                                        │   (Centifolia)
  │                      │                                                        │ Sweet Briar
  │                      │                                                        └ Tea
  │                      │
  │                      │                                                        ┌ Ayrshire
  │                      │                                                        │ Climbing Boursault
  │                      └ climbing                                              ┤ Climbing Tea
  │                                                                              │ Noisette
  │                                                                              └ Sempervirens
  │
  │                      ┌ non-climbing
  └ wild roses          ┤
                         └ climbing
```

some of the categories. Each group has its own characteristics, but those of soft colours and sweet scent which are most associated with old-fashioned roses are shared by many.

Wild roses or 'species' roses are the ancestors of all the modern and old garden roses. As might be expected, they are often vigorous and have rather sprawling growth. Although most have only a short flowering period, many make up for this with attractive foliage and hips in autumn.

Roses within these groups can have

different flower forms, and this gives rise to yet another set of descriptive terms used in books and catalogues: those most commonly used are illustrated in Figure 22.

Ways of using roses in the garden

No garden scheme need be without roses: in their various forms they can be equally appropriate to cottage gardens and formal parks. There are types suitable for bedding, for edging, for shrubberies, for mixed borders, for ground cover, for climbing up walls and over arches.

Rose beds

The tradition of planting bush roses in beds of their own persists for several good reasons. First of all, it makes maintenance easy: the heavy mulching in spring and frequent dead-heading in summer that roses need is more difficult to carry out in mixed beds. Roses also have most impact when grown in isolation: the mass of colour produced by the cluster-flowered types hardly needs any support, and somehow it is not easy to find plants that complement the rather uncompromising stance and perfect blooms of the large-flowered types. Against this, however, is the fact that the beds will look dull for at least half of the year.

So, large rose beds are not good value in the small garden – but are appropriate at the bottom of a large garden, for example, where they can be appreciated in the summer months. The essentials in planning such beds are, first, to plant in groups – say of three or five of one variety – and second, to keep unsympathetic colours apart. Consider even just using one or perhaps two varieties. The cluster-flowered roses are really *the* best for bedding, but the large-flowered types and some of the old 'China' roses are also suitable. Miniatures are

Single: less than 8 petals.

Semi-double: 8–20 petals.

Double: 20–40 petals.

High-centred and regular: 'hybrid T' type.

Split-centred where inner petals confused or sometimes split into four distinct quarters.

Figure 22. Types of rose flower.

especially useful in small gardens and raised beds. The different types tend not to mix well together, but often small shrub roses are included to give height in a large bed, and miniatures can be used for edging.

Some of the barren look of the beds in winter can be offset by underplanting or edging them with low-growing plants (edging has none of the drawbacks just mentioned). Suitable plants include violas, pinks, bugle, alpine strawberries and London pride, and with taller roses perhaps lady's mantle or catmint. Other possibilities are spring bulbs such as snowdrops, aconites and scillas, and dwarf shrubs such as winter-flowering heathers, thyme and artemesias.

Mixed borders

Some of the old garden roses, which are less formal than their modern counterparts and have softer colours, can blend well into a mixed border. Choose those that are not too big, and preferably are repeat-flowering – such as some of the China roses ('Bloomfield Abundance' and 'Cecile Brunner' are good examples). A few of the modern shrub roses such as 'Constance Spry' or 'Lavender Lassie' are also suitable for large borders.

The neighbouring plants must be carefully chosen, as the delicate rose blooms are easily overpowered. Foxgloves, campanulas, herbaceous geraniums, gypsophila and peonies fit in well, for example, whereas large scarlet poppies certainly do not!

Odd corners

In odd corners you could plant a large shrub rose, even in a small garden, and one of the bushier wild roses such as Rosa alba would be a good choice: this flowers in late June, has hips in autumn and in between its attractive foliage would form a good backdrop to two or three small repeat-flowering roses if there is room. Alternatively, you could choose one of the modern shrub roses for such a spot.

Shrubberies

Many shrub roses have at least as much to add to a mixed shrub border as most of the common flowering shrubs. In spring and late summer their leaves form an ideal background and in autumn any that produce hips add appropriately to the seasonal colour. Wild shrub roses can be planted in rough grass along with other vigorous shrubs.

Climbing and sprawling

House walls provide warmth and shelter, and the neater but stiffer modern climbers are most suitable here, together with a few of the less vigorous old climbers such as the 'noisette' Mme Alfred Carrière. These are also suitable for growing up posts and pillars. Rambler roses are good for training over arches, disguising old sheds and scrambling into trees. On walls they tend to look untidy and to suffer from mildew because of the dryness. Many climbers and ramblers can be trained along wires to provide attractive screens or dividers within the garden, although obviously they are not so effective in winter.

Roses are not usually thought of as 'ground cover' plants but a few do grow densely enough to suppress weeds and could usefully cover a difficult bank or unsightly mound, for example. For large areas Rosa × paulii is often recommended, and for small areas the Japanese rose 'Nozomi'.

Growing conditions

The conditions most roses need to give their *best* performance are:

Table 16: Roses for less than ideal conditions.

Shrub roses for partial shade	Poor soil	Vigorous modern bush roses
Alba roses: e.g.,	Alba roses: e.g.,	Alec's Red
Celestial	Celestial	Alexander
Great Maiden's Blush	Great Maiden's Blush	Anne Cocker
Queen of Denmark	Queen of Denmark	Elizabeth of Glamis
R. nitida	*R. gallica:*	Glenfiddich
	The wild roses and some	Honeymoon
North wall climbers	*gallica* old garden roses;	Iceberg
Alberic Barbier	e.g:	Queen Elizabeth
Golden Showers†	Complicata	Superstar
Hamburger Phoenix	Officinalis (Apothecary's	
Mme Alfred Carrière	rose)	
Mme Gregoire Staechelin*	Rosa mundi	
Sympathie	*R. rugosa* varieties; e.g.:	
	Alba	
	Frau Dagmar Hartopp	
	Roseraie de l'Hay	
	Scabrosa	
	Scotch roses:	
	Stanwell Perpetual	

* prone to mildew   † prone to blackspot

- good drainage
- plenty of light
- a deep rich soil

But these conditions are not so restricting as may first appear: by preparing the site well and choosing varieties carefully, it is possible to grow roses in all sorts of places. In a lot of ways they are tolerant plants. Many modern varieties put up with draughts and car fumes, for example, which makes them good for city gardens. The wild roses *R. rugosa* tolerate sandy soils and wind, so will flourish in seaside areas.

Good drainage, however, really is an essential: although roses need plenty of moisture, they do not like to be waterlogged. A site which is sunny for most of the day is ideal, but some roses will grow in a shadier place provided it is fairly open, and a few climbers will even do well on a north wall (see Table 16). However, avoid sites near large trees.

Soils can be improved by double digging, adding plenty of well-rotted compost or manure, and forking peat or leafmould into the surface before planting. Some of the wild and old garden roses are more tolerant of poor dry soils than the modern hybrids – if you want to try these in less than ideal conditions, choose the most vigorous varieties (Table 16).

Roses will tolerate some wind, the main danger being that it causes the roots to loosen; thus in exposed places use low-growing varieties and make sure you plant them firmly.

Roses planted on the site of an old rose bed, or specimen roses replaced in the same spot, never seem to thrive. The reason for this 'rose-sickness' is not fully understood, but such replanting is best avoided for several years after the old roses have been removed.

All season colour

Most modern roses and a few groups of

Table 17: Commonly available roses that are renowned for their scent.

Large-flowered
Alec's Red
Alpine Sunset
Champion
Ernest E. Morse
Fragrant Cloud*
Mme Butterfly
My Choice
Sweetheart
Tenerife
Wendy Cussons

Climbers and Ramblers
Albertine†
Compassion
Etoile de Hollande
Gloire de Dijon†
Mme Alfred Carrière
Mme Gregoire Staechelin†
New Dawn
Shot Silk
Zéphirine Drouhin†

Modern shrub roses
Chinatown
Constance Spry
Fountain
Fred Loads
Frühlingsgold
Golden Wings
Lavender Lassie

Cluster-flowered
Arthur Bell
English Miss
Fragrant Delight
Korresia
Margaret Merril
Scented Air

Old Garden Roses
Bourbon roses*: e.g.,
  Boule de Neige
Damask roses: e.g.,
  Mme Hardy
Gallica roses†: e.g.,
  Belle de Crécy
  Charles de Mills
Hybrid musks†: e.g.,
  Buff Beauty
  Cornelia
  Felicia
  Penelope
Moss roses†: e.g.,
  Common Moss
  White Bath

Species roses
R. alba: e.g.,
  Celestial
  Queen of Denmark
R. rubiginosa and some hybrids: e.g.,
  Lady Penzance
R. rugosa and some hybrids: e.g.,
  Frau Dagmar Hartopp
  Blanc Double de Coubert
  Roseraie de l'Hay
  Scabrosa
R. xanthina
  Canary Bird

* prone to blackspot   † prone to mildew

old roses are 'repeat-flowering' as already described – usually blooming from mid-summer to the first frosts. Some of the rest have two 'flushes', one in mid-summer and one in autumn, but many flower only once. This is certainly one of the first things to find out from a catalogue description.

The flowers come in every colour, except (despite some over-optimistic naming!) in shades of blue. There are strong bold reds and yellows and the most delicate pastel shades of pink and buff. There are also those which change from one colour to give two or three-tone effects as they open and mature; for example, the cluster-flowered 'Masquerade'.

Take account of the background when choosing climbers or roses for a border. White walls and wooden fences suit any colour, but some pinks and crimsons do not go well with red brick. An evergreen hedge makes an excellent background to bush roses.

Whereas few modern roses are of much interest when they are not in flower, many old garden roses have attractive foliage (the purple grey of *Rosa rubrifolia*, for example) and a few are almost evergreen. They often bear large scarlet or orange hips in autumn.

Scent
The old garden roses are unrivalled for fragrance. However, in recent years this quality has again become a priority of the rose breeders, with the result that several of the newer large-flowered bush roses are notably fragrant. The cluster-flowered ones are less so, and few modern shrub roses or miniatures have more than a faint scent. Scented climbers on a house wall are especially appreciated and here there is a fair choice. Some of the roses renowned for their scent are listed in Table 17. Less widely acclaimed are the roses with scented leaves: *Rosa primula*, for example, is often aptly called the 'Incense rose' because of the strong warm smell of its fern-like foliage, more noticeable after a shower of rain. *Rosa rubiginosa* 'Lady Penzance' also has scented leaves.

Wildlife
There are four roses native to Britain: *Rosa arvensis* (field rose), *Rosa canina* (dog rose), *Rosa rubiginosa* (sweet briar or eglantine) and *Rosa pimpinellifolium* (Scotch or burnet rose). The dog rose is cultivated mainly as a rootstock for modern roses, but garden forms of the last two species are available and of value. The sweet briar is particularly suitable for hedging, and Scotch roses form low growing, dense shrubs.

The native roses, and also wild roses introduced from other parts of the world, have single flowers, and these are the best for providing nectar for insects. Cultivated forms of these wild roses (and some of the old garden roses derived from them) often retain this feature. They also produce a fine autumn display of hips, varying from the tiny dark 'berries' of the Scotch roses to the 2 inch (5cm) long flask-shaped hips of *Rosa moyessii* – all appreciated by the birds in hard winter months.

Cutting
The near-perfect blooms of large-flowered bush roses with their long stiff stems are ideal for formal flower arrangements. Bushes earmarked for cutting can be 'disbudded' (Figure 23) to ensure large single blooms. These should be picked when the buds are just beginning to open. Do not cut off more than one-third of the flowering stem: removing too many leaves weakens the bush especially if it is newly planted. Some cluster-flowered roses are also recommended for cutting, but with these more unopened buds are

Table 18: A selection of roses good for cutting.

Large-flowered	Cluster-flowered
Alexander	Anne Cocker
Elizabeth Harkness	Arthur Bell
King's Ransom	Chanelle
Pascali	Iced Ginger
Silver Jubilee	Corp
Sunsilk	Margaret Merril
Superstar	Queen Elizabeth
	Southampton

wasted; the stems of the trusses are weaker so that the arrangement becomes less formal. All the varieties listed in Table 18 keep their petals and colour well, and there are many others that are equally good. Miniature roses can also be useful: they are ideal for buttonholes, for example.

The old garden roses drop their petals too quickly to be used in displays, but those that are highly scented have other uses in the house. The dried petals are the basis of many pot-pourri mixtures, and a syrup made from rose-water gives a delightful summer flavour to drinks, ice-cream and other sweets. The hips of wild roses are rich in vitamin C and can be collected to make rosehip syrup.

Buying roses

Although you will normally buy roses in the winter, summer is the time to start making your choice: try to see them flowering in gardens and nurseries, as no catalogue can describe the colour and fragrance accurately.

Garden centres may have plants that are container grown. These are relatively expensive, but can be planted at any time of year with care. Choose plants with plenty of sturdy stems. They should have been grown in the pots and not just put in them from open ground, so the roots should fill the containers.

Most plants are sold bare-rooted during the winter; either dug up from nursery beds or from temporary beds of peat at garden centres. If you buy them or they arrive through the post when the weather is unfit for planting, cover the roots in moist peat or sacking to prevent them drying out.

Be particularly wary of prepackaged roses sold in shops and supermarkets as they have often been kept in the warm too long. Do not buy them if you see that they have started to sprout.

Planting

Planting time

Bare-rooted plants can be put in any time from late October to March when the weather is suitable (not frosty or very wet); the best time is early November. Containerized plants can go in at any time, but will need copious watering in summer.

Spacing

Most bush roses should be planted 2 feet (60 cm) apart, although the smaller ones can go 18 inches (45cm) apart and the larger ones 3 feet (1m). Shrub roses need

Pinch out the side buds when they are still young, to give the main bud all the available food and growing space

When picking, cut just above a leaf joint

Figure 23. Roses for flower arrangements.

14. Large red autumn hips appear at the same time as a second flush of flowers on the wild *Rugosa* rose.

15. The colour of the shrubs in this mixed border determines the choice of predominantly yellow and red herbaceous plants and bulbs.

(a)

(b)

(c)

16. A new rose bed: (a) planting; (b) pruning and mulching; (c) first-year flowers.

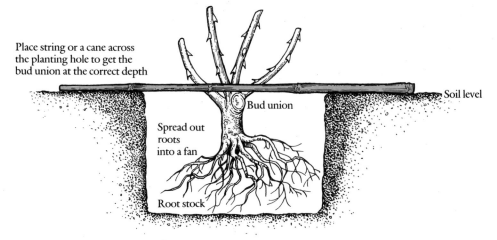

Place string or a cane across the planting hole to get the bud union at the correct depth

Soil level

Bud union

Spread out roots into a fan

Root stock

Figure 24. Planting bare-rooted bush roses.

4–6 feet (1.3–2m) and miniatures only about 1 foot (30cm). Climbers and ramblers should be set at intervals of at least 7 feet (1.6m), keeping them at least 1 foot (30cm) away from any wall or fence.

Planting method
Ideally the site should be prepared in late summer for winter planting by digging in plenty of compost or well-rotted manure; for single shrubs or climbers, try to prepare an area about 4 feet (1.3m) square.

When you come to plant, take out holes about 1 foot (30cm) square and 9 inches (23cm) deep – large enough to spread the roots of bare-rooted plants. Most modern roses are not growing on their own roots but are budded onto 'root stocks' (the roots of wild roses or their close relations) and this often gives an 'L' shaped root system. The bud union should be just below ground level when the rose is planted (Figure 24). Gradually fill in around the roots with a mixture of the top soil, a little peat and a small handful of bonemeal for each rose. Firm it well by treading lightly round the

plant – and repeat this after winter frosts if necessary.

Pruning and training
Good pruning can make all the difference to the health of roses, as well as giving you more and better blooms. All types need some attention but it is the modern bush roses and climbing types which benefit most. The general principles are simple:

1. Remove any dead, diseased or broken stems as these are obviously a health hazard.
2. Remove crossing and crowded shoots to allow light and air into the centre; always prune to just above an *outward*-pointing bud, or one pointing parallel to the wall in the case of climbers.
3. Remove very spindly shoots completely. Weak shoots should be cut back *more* severely than vigorous ones: this may seem wrong at first, but such pruning will encourage strong growth lower down the plant, while the taller shoots are held back by producing more side growths and blooms.

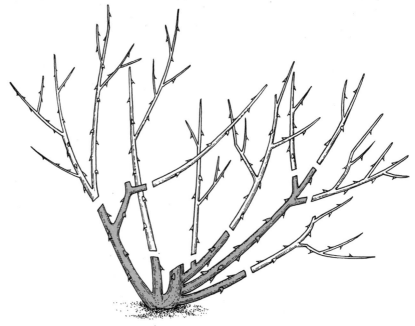

Figure 25. Pruning an established modern bush rose. (The broken lines indicate wood which is to be cut away.)

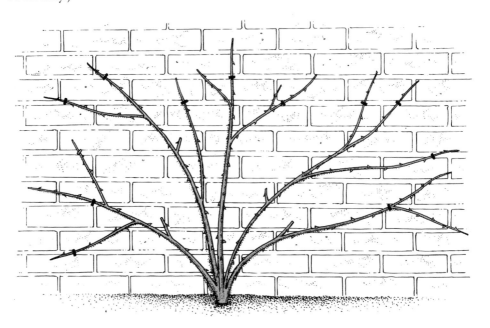

Figure 26. Training a climbing rose against a wall. Fan out the stems so that they are not vertical to encourage side shoots; tie in those that will contribute usefully to the main framework; cut the rest back to two or three buds.

Modern bush roses

In most parts of Britain, March or early April is the best time to prune modern bush roses – just as the top leaf buds are bursting. In warm sheltered spots where there is little likelihood of frost damage you can risk doing it earlier. First remove dead stems, etc. as explained above. Then, for large-flowered bushes, cut strong shoots back to about five buds on the old wood and weak ones to about three. For cluster-flowered types, which are more vigorous, prune similarly to within five and seven buds (Figure 25). Newly planted roses should be pruned hard – to within about four buds of the base of the bush.

Climbers and ramblers

In the spring after planting, clip the strongest growths of both climbers and ramblers to about 12–18 inches (30–45cm) and tie them in; cut the weak ones to about 3–4 inches (7.5–10cm) of the base.

With climbers, these growths form the start of a permanent framework and vigorous young shoots which appear during the summer should be tied in to extend it. The flowers are borne on short side shoots, which can be encouraged to occur by *bending* the main stems, arching them against a wall or weaving them around a pillar (Figure 26). The side shoots should be cut back to two or three buds in spring.

True ramblers have no permanent framework. They bear most flowers on new growth produced from the base during the previous summer – easily recognizable by its bright colour and flexibility. Ideally, you should cut all old stems that have flowered down to ground level in late summer and tie in the new ones. If there are not enough young growths to act as replacements, keep the best of the old stems for another year, pruning them like climbers. If new shoots are produced further up the plant, rather than from the base, cut the old wood back to this point.

If the lower part of old climbers or ramblers becomes bare, try cutting one or two old stems back hard to about 1 foot (30cm) from the base to encourage new growth.

Old and modern shrub roses

Less formal pruning is necessary with shrub roses. Cut out dead and congested growth as for all roses, but after this merely keep the shrubs shaped and within their allotted space. If the old stems start to become exhausted and bare at the base, cut one or two hard back each year to induce fresh growth.

Miniatures

Be cautious with miniature roses at first. Simply remove faded flowers, and dead or crossing branches. If they get too big, start pruning them like cluster-flowered varieties.

Care during the growing season

Mulching—Mulch round all plants in late spring, preferably with well-rotted manure or compost (see Chapter 2). Peat or leafmould can be used instead, but this will need the addition of a general organic feertilizer such as fish, blood and bone.

Feeding—The mulch should provide a lot of nutrients, but an annual boost of bonemeal (a small handful per plant) is often recommended.

Watering—All roses benefit from watering during dry summers, but those that are newly planted – especially climbers against walls – need most attention.

Weeding—Hoe or pull out annual weeds that grow through the mulch. Lift any perennial weeds gently with a fork, disturbing the bed as little as possible. Watch for 'suckers' growing out from the rootstock of modern roses (the leaves of these shoots are usually small and light green). Remove them by pulling gently rather than cutting.

Dead-heading—Faded flowerheads should be removed from all roses which bloom continuously or have a second flush of flowers in the autumn. Cut just above the the third or fourth leaf down the stem to produce a strong new flowering shoot. In exposed places, cut back the growth of tall roses by about one-third in late autumn so that they will not rock about in winter gales.

Pests and diseases

A formidable number of pests and diseases are often associated with roses, the most common of which are described in Chapter 2. In most gardens, however, only a few will reach a level that damages the appearance and health of the plants.

Diseases

The two main rose diseases – black spot and powdery mildew – are all too familiar, but can often be avoided by choice of variety and providing good growing conditions.

It is generally only the modern bush roses and some modern climbers that suffer from black spot, and there are varieties of these that are largely resist-

Table 19: The ten most disease-resistant modern bush roses – from an analysis by the Royal National Rose Society.

1.	Pink Favourite
2.	Silver Jubilee
3.	Peace
4.	Grandpa Dickson
5.	Red Devil
6.	Rose Gaujard
7.	Alexander
8.	Southampton
9.	Wendy Cussons
10.	Honey Favourite

ant: those in Table 19 are good examples, but there are many more. The 1950s rose 'Pink Favourite' is outstanding for its overall disease resistance, and some of the recent varieties are also likely to be good. On the other hand, the useful climber 'Golden Showers' is, unfortunately, particularly susceptible. Black spot is worse in hot wet weather, so avoid planting in closed-in areas, especially near dripping trees. (Such damp conditions are also the main cause of buds browning and dropping before they open.) The spores of the fungus overwinter on dead leaves, so remove these from the beds in autumn; mulching in the spring helps prevent reinfection from the soil.

Powdery mildew can affect all types of roses, but again there are resistant and susceptible varieties. The wild roses *R. rugosa* and *R. alba* and all their garden hybrids are scarcely ever affected, while rambler roses and many of the old garden *gallica* roses are particularly mildew-prone. The modern bush roses listed in Table 19 are not likely to suffer, but bad growing conditions can change this. Powdery mildew is aggravated by *dry* conditions and roses planted on poor, shallow soils are far more at risk; the fungus will also often attack soft lush growth such as may be caused by chemical nitrogen fertilizers.

Rose rust is another severe disease, but luckily much less common than black spot or mildew (see Table 2).

Die back of the tips of rose branches is often a sign of bad husbandry: it can occur if the roots are waterlogged or damaged by digging, or if fungi enter into wounded stems; it can also be caused by frost, and since young growth is most at risk, you should avoid using manure or fertilizers late in the season.

Unhealthy looking leaves are not necessarily symptoms of disease: they can be caused by a shortage of certain nutrients, bad drainage or frost damage. Yellow areas *between* the leaf veins are often a sign of iron, manganese or magnesium deficiency, particularly on a limy soil. Foliar feeding and mulching with compost and peat can help to correct this.

Pests

Although many common insect pests attack roses, usually incidents are only isolated and, for small numbers of roses, the general answer is to inspect them regularly and rely on picking the marauders off by hand or, alternatively, spray with derris. Caterpillars, sawfly, froghoppers and leafhoppers affect the leaves and shoots.; thrips and chafers affect the blooms (see Table 1).

The most unsightly attacker is likely to be the green or yellowish rose aphid. These often cover the buds and new shoots early in the summer, when few natural enemies of the aphid are about. Late summer blooms, when predators are more numerous, are less likely to be affected.

A selection of roses

Wild or species roses

R. MOYESII
A tall vigorous shrub, grown for its large flask-shaped hips as well as its flowers. The species is good for a large wild garden, but there are more compact varieties, e.g:

'Geranium'
Height—7 feet (2.1m), *spread* 5 feet (1.5m).
Flowers—Single, vivid red; June.

R. RUBRIFOLIA
The wild species forms a compact bush grown for its dusky purple foliage and red hips. The stems have few thorns.
Height and spread—5 feet (1.5m).
Flowers—Small, single, dark pink; June.

R. RUGOSA
Garden forms of the wild *R. rugosa* (native of China and Japan) form sturdy, hardy bushes which will grow on poor soils. They are very healthy: completely resistant to black spot and mildew. They have glossy green foliage in spring which turns gold in autumn, and most produce large orange-red hips. Good for specimen bushes and hedges, e.g:

'Alba'
Height and spread—5 feet (1.5m).
Flowers—Single, white, fragrant, appearing in June and then intermittently throughout the summer, followed by large hips.

'Frau Dagmar Hartopp'
Height— 4½ feet (1.4m), *spread* 3½ feet (1.1m).
Flowers—Single, shell pink, very fragrant, appearing in June and then intermittently until a second autumn flush, followed by large hips.

'Roseraie de l'hay'
Height and spread—7 feet (2.1m).
Flowers—Semi-double, deep red/purple, fragrant, repeat-flowering.

'Scabrosa'
Height 5 feet (1.5m), *spread* 6 feet (1.8m).
Flowers—Single, deep pink, fragrant, repeat-flowering, followed by large hips.

R. PRIMULA (Incense rose)
An upright shrub with ferny foliage that gives off a strong, warm scent when crushed or after rain.
Height and spread—8 feet (2.4m).
Flowers—Single, pale yellow, fragrant; May.

R. SPINOSISSIMA (Scotch or Burnet rose)
Garden varieties of the native rose and their hybrids form low thick bushes. They are hardy and will flourish on light

soils. Most have small round black hips, e.g:

'Stanwell Perpetual'
Height and spread—4 feet (1.2m).
Flowers—Semi-double, light pink, fragrant; May/June.

R. XANTHINA
An attractive arching bush with ferny foliage; useful as a specimen bush because of its early flowers, and also suitable for hedging, e.g:

'Canary Bird'
Height and spread—6 feet (1.8m).
Flowers—Single, clear yellow, fragrant; May.

Climbers and ramblers
ALBERIC BARBIER
A vigorous old rambler, useful because it will flourish in poor conditions with little direct sunlight. Foliage is almost evergreen. Suitable for an arch or screen rather than a wall.
Height—20 feet (6.3m).
Flowers—Double, cream, formed in clusters, fragrant; June–July.

ALOHA
A slow-growing climber, good for small walls and pillars. Disease and weather resistant.
Height—8 feet (2.4m).
Flowers—Double (large-flowered type), deep pink, fragrant; repeat flowering.

ALTISSIMO
A healthy short climber with very attractive single flowers. Good for walls, pillars and fences.
Height—8 feet (2.4m).
Flowers—Large, single, blood-red, slightly fragrant; repeat flowering.

COMPASSION
A short climber, very free flowering, suitable for pillars or walls.
Height—8 feet (2.4m).

Flowers—Double, well-shaped, pink-apricot, very fragrant; repeat flowering.

COMPLICATA
An old gallica rose, also grown as a shrub.
Height—7 feet (2.1m).
Flowers—Very large, single, rich pink, slightly fragrant; mainly June/July.

MME ALFRED CARRIÈRE
A vigorous old climber, suitable for a north wall.
Height—20 feet (6.3m).
Flowers—Double, white with a pink flush, very fragrant; repeat flowering.

NEW DAWN
A rambler, but one that is a lot less rampant than many and is repeat flowering – suitable for hedges, arches and climbing into trees rather than walls.
Height—10 feet (3m).
Flowers—Small, semi-double, pink, fragrant; repeat flowering.

SCHOOLGIRL
A healthy climber, suitable for walls or screens.
Height—10 feet (3m).
Flowers—Double (large-flowered type), dusky orange, fragrant; repeat flowering.

SYMPATHIE
A tough disease-resistant climber that will grow on a north wall.
Height—12 feet (3.7m).
Flowers—Double, bright red, fragrant; repeat flowering.

VEILCHENBLAU
A rambler with fairly restrained growth and unusual flower colour. Good for growing over arches and screens.
Height—14 feet (4.3m).

Flowers—Small, semi-double in large clusters, violet with a pale centre, fragrant; June–July.

Old garden roses
ALBA ROSES
These are all robust hardy shrubs, thriving in adverse conditions and resistant to disease. They have grey-green leaves on stems with few prickles. Good for training against trellises, as hedges or as specimen bushes, e.g:

'Celestial'
Height—6 feet (1.8m), *spread* 4 feet (1.2m).
Flowers—Double, soft pink, fragrant; late June and July.

'Maiden's Blush'
Height—6 feet (1.8m), *spread* 5 feet (1.5m).
Flowers—Double, rich pink softening with age, fragrant; late June and July.

'Queen of Denmark'
Height—5 feet (1.5m), *spread* 4 feet (1.2m).
Flowers—Double, pink, very fragrant; late June and July.

CHINA ROSES
China roses are among the few old garden roses that are repeat flowering. They generally form low open bushes with clusters of small flowers; they are fairly disease resistant, but do best in a sunny position. Good for rose beds and mixed borders. Varieties still commonly available include the following:

'Bloomfield Abundance'
Height and spread—6 feet (1.8m).
Flowers—Double, shell pink, slightly fragrant; repeat flowering from June.

'Cecile Brunner'
Height and spread—2½ feet (0.75m).
Flowers—Double, shell pink fading to white, slightly fragrant; repeat flowering.

'Perle d'Or'
Height—4 feet (1.2m), *spread* 3 feet (0.9m).
Flowers—Double, apricot fading to cream, slightly fragrant; repeat flowering.

SWEET BRIARS
These are hybrids of the native *R. rubiginosa* and are grown for their fragrant foliage and hips as well as their flowers, e.g:

'Lady Penzance'
Height and spread—6 feet (1.8m).
Flowers—Single, copper-coloured, very fragrant; June.

Modern shrub roses
CHINA TOWN
A healthy, tolerant, large bush rose (sometimes classified as a cluster-flowered rose). Good for hedging or the back of a border.
Height—5 feet (1.5m), *spread* 4 feet (1.2m).
Flowers—Double, yellow with a pink tinge, fragrant; repeat flowering.

FOUNTAIN
A healthy upright shrub, dark foliage.
Height—5 feet (1.5m), *spread* 3 feet (1.0m).
Flowers—Double (large-flowered type), blood red, fragrant; repeat flowering.

FRED LOADS
A healthy vigorous shrub, very free-flowering. Good as a specimen shrub.
Height—6 feet (1.8m), *spread* 4 feet (1.2m).
Flowers—Large, single, vermilion, fragrant; repeat flowering.

FRÜHLINGSGOLD
A large shrub with arching branches. Healthy and easy to grow. An impress-ive early-flowering specimen bush for a

large garden.
Height and spread—7 feet (2.1m).
Flowers—Large, semi-double, light gold, fragrant; May.

GOLDEN WINGS
A useful, very healthy shrub; suitable for a specimen bush.
Height—6 feet (1.8m), *spread* 5 feet (1.5m).
Flowers—Large, single, yellow; repeat flowering.

LAVENDER LASSIE
A disease-resistant shrub; its clusters of flowers stand up well to rain. Suitable for a specimen bush.
Height—4½ feet (1.4m), *spread* 3½ feet (1.1m).
Flowers—Double, rosette-shaped, lilac pink, fragrant; repeat flowering.

Large-flowered bush roses (hybrid teas)
These roses have been selected for their vigour, disease resistance and, where possible, fragrance over a wide colour range. They are all repeat flowering.

ALEC'S RED
Vigorous, sweetly scented; flowers stand up well to rain.
Height—3 feet (1m).
Flowers—Light crimson, very fragrant.

ALPINE SUNSET
Sturdy, sweet scented.
Height—2½ feet (0.75m).
Flowers—Peach coloured, very fragrant.

CHAMPION
Height—2½ feet (0.75m).
Flowers—Creamy pink with a gold flush, very fragrant.

ERNEST H. MORSE
One of the most healthy deep red roses;

blooms weather well.
Height—3 feet (1m).
Flowers—Dark red, very fragrant.

KING'S RANSOM
Flowers abundantly; well-shaped rain-resistant blooms; recommended for cutting.
Height—2½ feet (0.75m).
Flowers—Pure yellow, fragrant.

PEACE
A larger than average bush rose, vigorous and generally disease resistant.
Height—4½ feet (1.4m).
Flowers—Large, yellow edged with pink, slightly fragrant.

SILVER JUBILEE
One of the most disease resistant roses, producing abundant blooms.
Height—2½ feet (0.75m).
Flowers—Large, coral pink, fragrant.

WENDY CUSSONS
Tall for a bush rose. Blooms highly scented and weather well.
Height—3½ feet (1.1m).
Flowers—Deep pink, very fragrant.

Cluster-flowered bush roses (floribundas)
Again chosen for colour, scent and disease resistance. All have the double high-centred flower shape typical of modern bush roses, unless stated otherwise.

ARTHUR BELL
One of the most fragrant floribundas, healthy and weather resistant. Good for bedding.
Height—3½ feet (1.1m).
Flowers—Large, golden yellow, very fragrant.

ENGLISH MISS
Vigorous bushes producing trusses of

small tight flowers. Good for bedding.

Height—2½ feet (0.75m).

Flowers—Small, delicate pink, very fragrant.

ESCAPADE

Healthy bushes producing flat blooms of unusual colouring. Good for bedding and mixed borders.

Height—2½ feet (0.75m).

Flowers—Semi-double, magenta with a white eye, musk scented.

FRAGRANT DELIGHT

Height—2½ feet (0.75m).

Flowers—Double, well-shaped, coppery pink, very fragrant.

MARGARET MERRIL

One of the most healthy white roses.

Good for bedding.

Height—3 feet (1m).

Flowers—Well-shaped, pearly white, very fragrant.

SCENTED AIR

Suitable for large beds.

Height—3 feet (1m).

Flowers—Large, pale scarlet, very fragrant.

SOUTHAMPTON

One of the most healthy floribundas; a good colour but not much scent. Suitable for large beds and for hedging.

Height—3½ feet (1.1m).

Flowers—Apricot orange, slightly fragrant.

CHAPTER 8
DRAWING UP PLANS

When you have a list of which flowers you would like to grow, and which are suited to the growing conditions in your garden, it is helpful to make a sketch of your proposed planting plan.

Measure the area to be planted, with a tape or by pacing it out: do not automatically assume that the boundaries are parallel or at right angles – they can be very deceptive. Make sure you know which direction is south. Transfer the outline onto paper, working to a scale: 1 inch = 2 feet (5cm = 1m) is a manageable one if your plot is about 20 feet (6m) long. Mark on the plan features such as trees and existing paths that you want to keep, and also indicate anything outside the garden which is relevant – causing shade or providing shelter.

The growing conditions which the plant needs primarily dictate its position but there are other factors such as its colour, height, flowering time and leaf form which you have to manipulate in order to get the best effect; thus you should note down this information for each plant on your list.

It is not easy to portray all these aspects on a plan. Using coloured pencils obviously helps. You could also try cutting out a small piece of paper for each plant and writing on its main features: the plan then becomes a jigsaw in space and time! Alternatively, use overlays on tracing paper – one for each of the seasons.

In a small garden it is possible to miss out the 'drawing board' stage and start directly outside marking out beds with string or a hose pipe (good for making curves), and moving pots and buckets about to represent the plants. However, it is not so easy to formulate completely new ideas like this as it is when faced with a blank outline on paper.

Keep your plan simple at first. As emphasized in earlier chapters, all plants look better in groups of one type rather than dotted here and there. Separate those with spectacular blooms by interspersing them with foliage plants, 'quieter' plants such as astrantia or plants which flower much earlier or later, otherwise they will lose much of their dramatic effect.

Even when there are many different types of plant in a small area, you can achieve a united effect with a careful colour scheme. This will often be influenced by existing features: a red brick wall, for example, would suggest schemes based on blues and whites. Pinks and mauves would be better against a background of grey or coppery shrubs such as a smoke bush (*Cotinus*), white variegated dogwood (*Cornus alba* 'Elegantissima') and purple sage (*Salvia officinalis* 'Purpurea'). Shrubs with bright green or yellow variegated leaves – *Elaeagnus pungens* 'Maculata' and *Salvia officinalis* 'Icterina', for example – would complement flowers that are orange, red or yellow.

These warm colours are enhanced by sunlight, whereas whites, pale yellows and pale blues stand out better in shadier places and in the evening.

Most people want a variety of different colours in their gardens and would not wish to copy the monochrome borders of some of the grand country houses. However, even in a small garden, there is a lot to be said for sticking to, say, a simple scheme of pastel colours. In a larger garden where there is room to introduce an element of surprise with hedges or screens, you could go further towards planting areas in just one or two colours.

Height is a fairly obvious factor to deal with, although it is sometimes the height of the *foliage* that dictates the position of a plant rather than that of its flowers. For example, a campanula that has low rosettes of leaves and narrow spikes of flowers can be used at the front of a border whereas a bushy plant of the same height could not. Although it is desirable to have plants of various heights arranged so that they are all visible, avoid the regimented look of long straight lines of equal height. The flowering time is also relevant here. For example, spring flowers such as primulas and lungwort can go at the back of a border even though they are small because most herbaceous plants will only just have begun to grow when they are in bloom.

The overall shape of many herbaceous perennials tends to be humpy and the spikes of red hot pokers, day lilies and many bulbous plants provide valuable contrast. There are similar contrasts in texture. The feathery foliage and frothy flowers of gypsophila have an abandoned air, and will successfully disguise fading clumps of flowers in a border. On the other hand, plants with large solid leaves, such as bergenia, can be relied upon to sit tidily next to a path.

These few suggestions may not be directly relevant to your own garden, but should be sufficient to alert you to the value of plant associations – in colour, form and texture. Look out for appealing combinations when you visit other gardens or even in the wild – some of the best can occur by accident! Above all, start trying out your ideas. During the flowering season, note down your successes and failures, which plants need moving and where the gaps are. You can always try again.

Flowers in a 'cottage' garden

The cottager's garden was traditionally at the front of his dwelling, the back being taken up with hens and animals. A central path led to the door, and on either side was an informal mixture of vegetables, fruit and flowers. This is an idea not to be ignored today, as a relief from unused front lawns and bedding plants, but is equally applicable to a back garden.

Nearly all the cottage garden flowers were hardy. Those brought in from the wild intermingled with occasional more exotic varieties passed on from the grand manor houses. They had to include those that were useful as well as decorative – particularly herbs for cooking and medicinal use, and simple colourful scented flowers loved by bees. Many seeded themselves, thereby producing the random appearance of the garden.

There are still plenty of these traditional varieties of flowers available today: hardy annuals, biennials, herbaceous perennials and bulbs. Most of those chosen here were introduced not later than the early nineteenth century. Although you may have to compromise a little with modern varieties, you should be able to avoid large-flowered and double-flowered hybrids. Producing an uncontrived appearance without ending up with a jungle is not always so easy!

Key to cottage garden plan

1. Hedges

    Hawthorn or mixed native shrubs
    Bushes near gate of holly or box

2. Climbing plants

    Plants for round the door and windows, or for climbing up any stumps or pillars in the garden:
    Honeysuckle – *Lonicera periclymenum*
    Everlasting pea – *Lathyrus latifolius*
    Jasmine – *Jasminum officinale*
    Clematis – small flowered varieties
    Roses – climbing roses with informal growth and flower shape. 'New Dawn' would go well over a porch.

3. Flowering shrubs

    Lilac – *Syringa vulgaris*
    Philadelphus – single flowered varieties
    Alba roses; e.g. 'Maiden's Blush'

4. Apple trees in rough grass with spring flowers

    Daffodils, preferably *Narcissus pseudonarcissus* or other small-flowered varieties
    Wood anemones – *Anemone nemerosa*
    Bluebells – *Endymion nonscriptus*
    Primroses – *Primula vulgaris*
    Sweet rocket – *Hesperis matronalis* ⎫ against
    Honesty – *Lunaria biennis* ⎬ hedge

5. Soft fruit

    Currant bushes, raspberries, rhubarb interspersed with spring bulbs and creeping herbaceous plants
    Snowdrop – *Galanthus nivalis*
    Snowflakes – *Leucojum* sp
    Star-of-Bethlehem – *Ornithogalum* sp
    Violet – *Viola odorata*
    Dead nettle – *Lamium* sp
    Bugle – *Ajuga* sp
    Lily-of-the-valley – *Convallaria* (in shaded corner)

6. Front border

    Pasque flower – *Pulsatilla vulgaris* ⎫
    Forget-me-not – *Myosotis sylvatica* ⎬ spring
    Lungwort – *Pulmonaria officinalis* ⎭

Hollyhock – *Althaea rosea*
Candytuft – *Iberis sempervirens*
Valerian – *Centranthus ruber*
Old-fashioned pink – *Dianthus* sp
Iris – *Iris germanica*

7. Herb bed containing wild herbs such as:

Comfrey – *Symphytum officinalis*
Mullein – *Verbascum*
Heartsease – *Viola tricolor*
Meadowsweet – *Filipendula ulmaria*

Together with the better known herbs introduced by the Romans such as marjoram, rosemary, savory, parsley, thyme, fennel, lavender and hyssop

8. (a) and (b): Vegetable plots

Contain some self-seeded annuals such as:
Poached-egg flower – *Limnanthes douglasii*
Marigold – *Calendula officinalis*
Heartsease – *Viola tricolor*

(c): Trellis of 'old-fashioned' sweet peas

9. Long borders either side of path
Herbaceous perennials:
Old-fashioned pink – *Dianthus* sp
Yarrow – *Achillea millefolium*
Columbine – *Aquilegia vulgaris*
Japanese anemone – *Anemone japonica*
Peony – *Paeonia* sp
Cranesbill – *Geranium* sp
Christmas and Lenten rose – *Helleborus* sp
Catmint – *Nepeta* × *faassenii*
Michaelmas daisy – *Aster novi-belgii*

Bulbs:
Lily – *Lilium regale*
Crocus – *C. chrysanthus*

Annuals and biennials:
Canterbury bell – *Campanula medium*
Mignonette – *Reseda odorata*
Foxglove – *Digitalis purpurea*
Sweet william – *Dianthus barbatus*
Love-in-a-mist – *Nigella damascena*

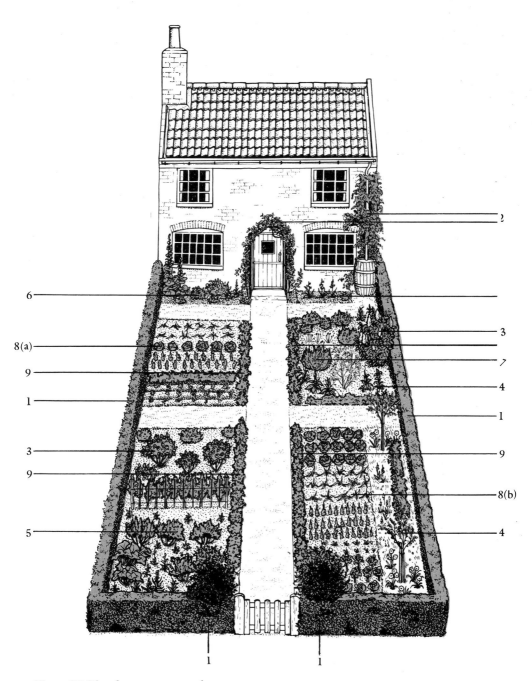

Figure 27. Plan for a cottage garden.

Figure 28. Plan for a terrace garden.

Flowers on a terrace

A terrace is used throughout the year – in summer almost as an extension to the house – which makes tidy, fairly formal planting appropriate. It is a good place for tubs and troughs, since here watering is easy and less likely to be forgotten. It should be warm and sheltered, so that you can grow less hardy plants, but this may mean it often gets hot and dry in summer.

One of the best schemes is to have small evergreen shrubs or neat herbaceous perennials which keep a low mat of foliage in winter and use them as a framework for seasonal bedding plants and bulbs. The terrace is a place where fragrance and form will be most appreciated.

Key to terrace plan

Varieties are chosen for pastel colours (pink, white and blue) but could be adapted for another colour scheme.

Permanent planting:

1. Climbing roses; e.g. 'Aloha' or 'Altissimo' – summer flowers
2. *Bergenia crassifolia* – early spring flowers
3. Rosemary – *Rosemarinus officinalis* ⎫ late spring
4. London pride – *Saxifraga* × *urbium* ⎬ flowers
5. Ice plant – *Sedum spectabile* ⎫ autumn
6. Japanese anemone – *Anemone* × *hybrida* ⎬ flowers

Spring bedding plants and bulbs for pots and spaces in beds:

Snowdrop – *Galanthus nivalis* 'S. Arnott' (scented)

Naturalized tulip – *Tulip kaufmanniana* 'Cesar Franck'

Dwarf forget-me-not – *Myosotis* 'Dwarf royal blue'

Grape hyacinth – *Muscaria* sp

Summer and autumn bedding and bulbs:

Petunia – single coloured 'multiflora' varieties; e.g. 'White joy', and 'Pink joy', for pots and spaces in beds

Alyssum – *Alyssum maritimum*; e.g. 'Snowdrift' for pots and spaces round rosemary bushes

Tobacco plant – *Nicotiana affinis*, for back of borders against hedge

Nerine – *Nerine bowdenii*, for spaces in beds

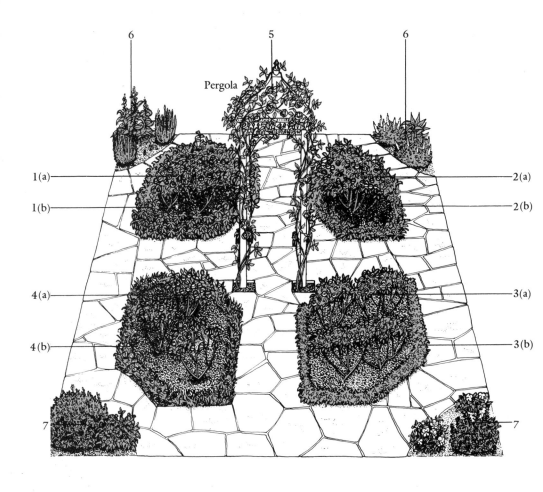

Figure 29. Plan for a formal rose garden.

A formal rose garden

The major disadvantage of modern shrub roses is their lack of winter interest. This can be partially compensated for in a formal rose garden by an attractive design of beds and paving. In addition edging plants can be used round the beds and surrounding walls to add some all-year-round colour.

Such a garden would be suitable for a town front garden – particularly since most roses are tolerant of the pollution from busy roads. It would be equally appropriate as a smaller part of a large back garden.

Key to rose garden plan

Cluster-flowered roses are the most effective for bedding. The four for this garden are chosen from the selection of disease-resistant and scented varieties in Chapter 7. Their colours combine well and they are approximately the same height. Other combinations from the list could be equally satisfactory.

Rose variety	Edging
1. (a) 'Arthur Bell'	(b) Lady's mantle – *Alchemilla*
2. (a) 'Southampton'	(b) Catmint – *Nepeta*
3. (a) 'Margaret Merril'	(b) Garden pink – *Dianthus*
4. (a) 'Scented air'	(b) Alpine strawberry

Pergola:

5. Climbing rose 'Compassion'

Corner beds:

6. Shrubby silver-leaved plants such as artemesias, thymes, lavender, and rosemary. Crocuses for spring.
7. Shade-loving evergreen shrubs such as Mexican orange blossom (*Choisya ternata*) and herbaceous plants such as hellebores and sweet violets.

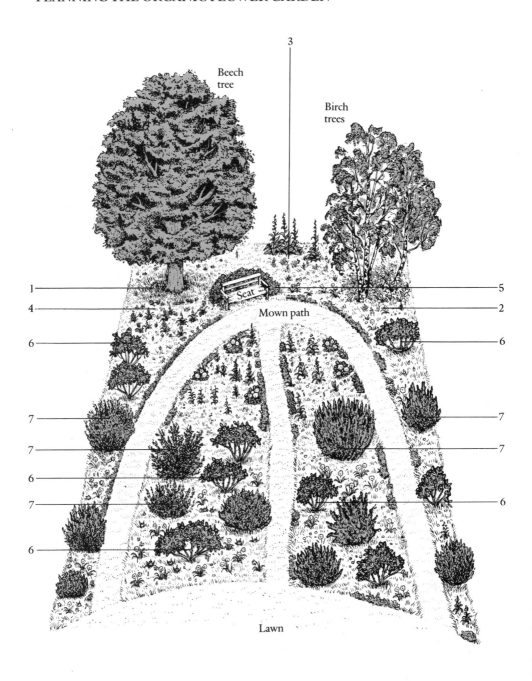

Figure 30. Plan for a wild garden.

Flowers in the wild garden

In a large garden it may be beneficial to have a 'wild area', where hardy plants grow in a natural way: under trees or through grass, ivy or ground cover plants. An area consisting of dappled shade under trees, together with shrubs in roughly mown grass which gradually becomes a tightly mown lawn is ideal. Native plants are obviously well-suited to such places, but wild areas also provide an opportunity to grow other garden plants that are too rampant for formal flower beds.

'Wild' in this case does not mean 'neglected' – as this part of the garden may need almost as much care as a herbaceous border to prevent it becoming untidy. For example, some of the flowers will spread quickly and any one species must be prevented from taking over.

Key to wild garden plan

1. Area close to trunk of large beech tree:

   Hardy cyclamen – *C. purpurascens*
   C. hederifolium
   C. coum

   Winter aconite –
   E. hyemalis
   Snowdrop – } early
   Galanthus sp } flowering
   Squill – } bulbs
   Scilla sp
   Violet – *Viola odorata*

2. Area under birch trees:

   Ground cover plants like *Symphytum grandiflorum* and *Geranium microrrhizum*. Daffodils (*Narcissus* sp) growing through.
   Solomon's seal – *Polygonatum bistorta*
   Martagon lily – *Lilium martagon*
   Primrose – *Primula* sp – on edge
   Stinking hellebore – *Helleborus foetidus*

3. Woodland grasses with:

   Wood anemone – *Anemone nemorosa*
   Bluebell – *Endymion* sp
   Foxglove – *Digitalis purpurea*

4. Rough grass (mown June–August) with spring and autumn bulbs:

   Dutch crocus – *C. vernus* hybrids
   Daffodil – *Narcissi*; e.g. 'Golden harvest', 'Beersheba'
   Spring snowflake – *Leucojum vernum*
   Star-of-Bethlehem – *Ornithogalum* sp
   Meadow saffron – *Colchicum* sp
   Autumn crocus – *Crocus speciosus*
   Primroses on edge.

5. Glade:

   Seat with 'bed' of self-sown flowers:
   Honesty – *Lunaria biennis*
   Sweet rocket – *Hesperis matronalis*
   Evening primrose – *Oenothera biennis*

   Late-mown grassy patch containing:
   Summer snowflake – *L. aestivum*
   Snake's head fritillary – *Fritillaria meleagris*
   Primulas on edge, plus some summer wild flowers.

6. Old garden roses and species roses:

   Any from selection in Chapter 7 depending on size of area. Some early flowering daffodils and Dutch crocuses.

7. A selection of shrubs, including some for autumn and winter colour, e.g:
   Holly – *Viburnum tinus*
   Witchhazel – *Hamamelis*
   Berberis – various species depending on size of area
   Viburnum – *Viburnum fragrans*
   Smoke bush – *Cotinus coggygria*

   and some for late summer flowers; e.g:
   Buddleia davidii

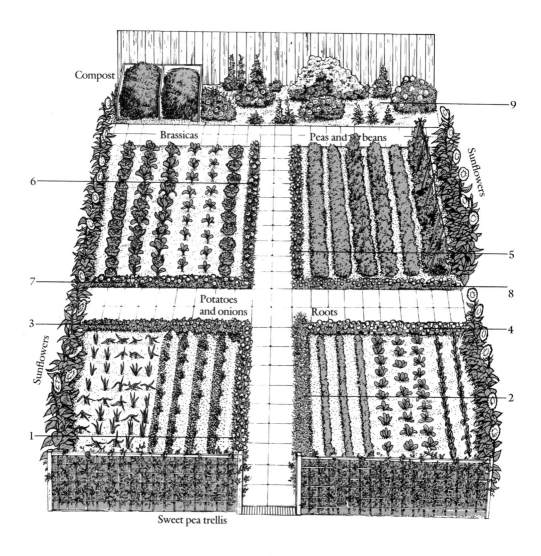

Figure 31. Plan for flowers in the vegetable garden.

Flowers in the vegetable garden

There are several reasons for growing flowers on a plot intended primarily for vegetables. First of all, of course, they make it look more attractive: this is particularly important in a small garden. Then there is the idea that flowers benefit the vegetable crops by attracting bees, which help pollination, and predators of insect pests. Increasing the diversity of the garden can in itself help reduce pests and disease attack (see Chapter 2). Traditionally, flowers for the house are grown in the vegetable garden so that cutting them does not spoil the main display. Annuals and half-hardy bulbs fit well into the rotation of vegetable crops – either on a patch of their own or as edging to the vegetable plots. Odd corners can be put down to more permanent herbaceous plants and the more rampant annuals: here tall varieties can be grown and easily staked. Some flowers such as nasturtiums and pot marigolds have an extra qualification for inclusion as they are edible.

Key to vegetable garden plan

Boundaries – sweet peas (*Lathyrus odoratus*) on trellis and giant sunflowers (*Helianthus annus*) against fence.

1. Sweet william – *Dianthus barbatus*
2. Gypsophila – *Gypsophila elegans*
3. Poached egg flower – *Limnanthes douglasii*
4. Nasturtium – *Tropaeolum majus*
5. Canterbury bell – *Campanula medium*
6. Love-in-a-mist – *Nigella damascena*
7. Pot marigold – *Calendula officinalis*
8. Baby-blue eyes – *Nemophila insignis*
9. Bed of herbaceous perennials for cutting, e.g:
   Lady's mantle – *Alchemilla mollis*
   Shasta daisy – *Chrysanthemum maximum*
   Korean chrysanthemum – *C. rubellum*
   Leopard's bane – *Doronicum plantagineum*

plus self-sown annuals such as honesty (*Lunaria biennis*)

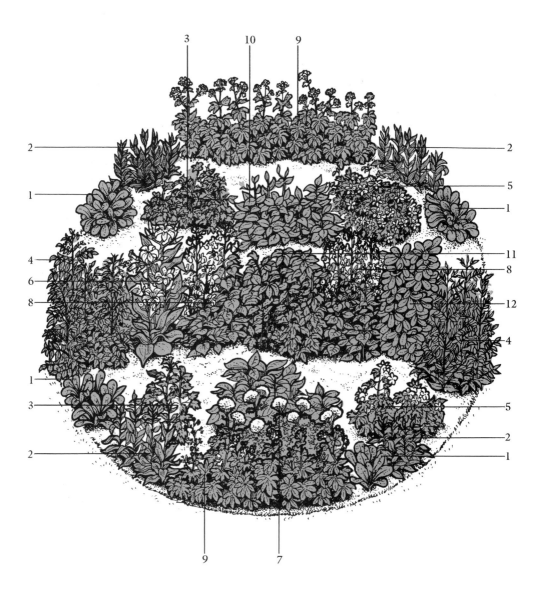

Figure 32. Plan for a herbaceous island bed – diameter approx. 10 feet (3.3m).

A herbaceous island bed

Herbaceous beds and borders have gone out of fashion — mostly because they lack interest in winter and because of the work involved in staking and dead-heading.

However, a herbaceous bed does establish quickly, and with a good choice of plants it can look neat and attractive — if not showy — for a good part of the year. It can be well cared for because the plants can be lifted and divided without disturbing more permanent shrubs or bulbs. The best flowers for such a bed are those which have attractive and lasting foliage, and that need no staking.

An island bed in a sheltered spot can often be more successful than a border against a wall or hedge, because there is less tendency for the plants to become drawn and dry, and the good air circulation minimizes the risk of disease.

Key to island bed plan

Varieties are chosen for a yellow/blue/pink colour scheme.

Spring/early summer:

1. Primrose – *Primula vulgaris*
2. Lungwort – *Pulmonaria* sp
3. Columbine – *Aquilegia* hybrids
4. Catmint – *Nepeta* × *faassenii*

Summer:

5. Cranesbill – *Geranium* 'Johnson's Blue'
6. Day lily – *Hemerocallis* 'Golden Chimes'
7. Yarrow – *Achillea* 'Moonshine'
8. *Salvia superba*
9. Lady's mantle – *Alchemilla vulgaris*

Late summer/autumn:

10. *Aster amellus* 'King George'
11. Japanese anemone – *Anemone* × *hybrida*
12. Ice plant – *Sedum spectabile*

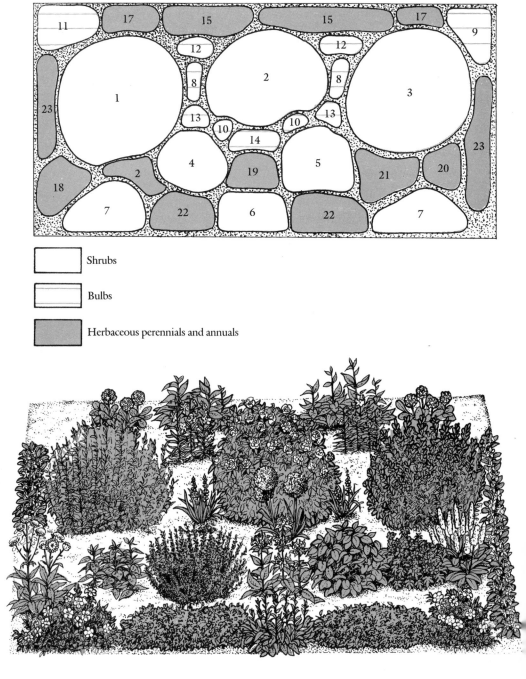

Shrubs

Bulbs

Herbaceous perennials and annuals

Figure 33. Plan for a mixed border – size approx. 18 feet × 8 feet (6m × 2.6m).

A mixed border

Borders containing a mixture of all different types of plants – shrubs, herbaceous plants, bulbs and perhaps even bedding plants and annuals – are now very popular. The days when most gardens had space for separate beds of each type have long since passed, and mixed borders are an easy way of providing colour and interest all year round. They require less maintenance than herbaceous borders or areas of bedding, and give shelter to tall and tender plants. Care is needed in planning and planting, however; there is always a danger of overcrowding the border, and of damaging shrub roots and bulbs when adding annuals or dividing perennials.

A mixed border is appropriate for any scale: from one with small shrubs, miniature bulbs and dwarf varieties of herbaceous plants, to a large border containing some small trees. Both mixed colour borders and those based around just one or two colours can be effective, as long as there is a balance of colour throughout the border during each season.

Shrubs form the framework, and are the main source of winter height and colour. Height can also be provided by climbers such as clematis and roses trained up stout posts. In spring, bulbs will be the most important – kept towards the back of the border where their dying leaves will be hidden. Herbaceous perennials then take over as the source of colour, but it is those with attractive shapes and foliage rather than showy flowers which blend in most successfully.

Hardy annuals, biennials and bedding plants can also be useful in a mixed border, particularly in its early years when the shrubs are small. Again it is the 'quieter' types that are the most suitable: like forget-me-nots, tobacco plants, pansies, nemophila, foxgloves and mignonette. Other solutions for gap-filling are ground cover perennials such as *Geranium microrrhizum* and *Symphytum grandiflorum*, or short-lived shrubs such as the decorative sages.

Key to mixed border plan
Shrubs:

1. Dogwood (purple stemmed – *Cornus alba* 'Sibirica' (winter colour)
2. Shrub rose, e.g: 'Bloomfield abundance' or 'Complicata' (summer flowers)
3. Smoke bush – *Cotinus coggyria* (autumn colour)
4. *Skimmia japonica* (evergreen, autumn berries)
5. *Berberis darwinii* (evergreen, spring flowers)
6. Purple sage – *Salvia officinalis* 'Purpurea' (evergreen)
7. *Potentilla fruticosa* (evergreen, summer flowers)

Bulbs:

8. Narcissi, e.g: 'Pheasant's Eye'
9. *Iris reticulata*
10. *Crocus chrysanthus*
11. Summer snowflake – *Leucojum aestivum*
} spring flowering

12. Lily, e.g: *Lilium regale, Lilium* 'Corsage'
13. Summer hyacinth – *Galtonia candicans*
14. *Allium albopilsum*
} summer flowering

Herbaceous plants:

15. Comfrey – *Symphytum grandiflorum*
16. Lungwort – *Pulmonaria saccharata*
} spring flowers

17. Primula
18. Astrantia
19. Bergamot – *Monarda*
   'Croftway Pink' } summer
20. Bistort – *Polygonum*   flowers
   bistorta
21. *Geranium microrrhizum*

22. Dwarf Michaelmas daisy – *Aster
   Novi-belgii* (autumn flowers)

Annuals:

23. Pansy – *Viola* × *wittrockiana*

FURTHER INFORMATION

Understanding plant names

Two useful books are:

Plant Names Simplified: their pronunciation, derivation and meaning, by A. T. Johnson and H. A. Smith. (Landsmans Bookshop Ltd, Buckenhill, Bromyard, Herefordshire).

Nuttalls Dictionary of Botanical Names, by E. Sandford (Frederick Warne, 1979).

Visiting gardens

The National Gardens Scheme,
57 Lower Belgrave Street,
London SW1W 0LR

Through The National Gardens Scheme many private gardens, large and small, are open to the public on certain days throughout the year in aid of charity. A national handbook, *Gardens of England and Wales Open to the Public,* giving dates and times is published every spring; many counties also publish their own list, and gardens are advertised locally.

Organic gardening

Henry Doubleday Research
Association,
National Centre for Organic
Gardening,
Ryton-on-Dunsmore,
Coventry CV8 3LG.

The HDRA is an organization to help amateur gardeners; they have a mail-order list of products and books on organic gardening. The National Centre includes 9 acres of demonstration gardens – fruit, flowers and vegetables.

INDEX